Heavy-type numerals denote chapter location

Queen's Island

0 ___ ½
Mile

Belfast 1885

a   Town Hall
b   Northern Counties Railway Station
c   Belfast and County Down Railway Station
d   Great Northern Station
e   York Street Mill
f   Harland & Wolff
g   Boyne Bridge
h   Durham Street
i   North Queen Street
j   Poor House
k   Castle Junction
l   RBAI (Inst)
m   St George's Church, High Street
n   Lagan river
o   Linen Hall

Heavy-type numerals denote chapter location

0 ___ 1
Mile

Parks

Belfast 1985

a   City Hall
b   Cave Hill
c   Cavehill Waterworks
d   Shaneen Park
e   Stormont

Inner boxed area: maps 1685 and 1785
Outer boxed area: map 1885

BELFAST
1000 YEARS

Jonathan Bardon
and Stephen Conlin

The
Blackstaff Press

To Mary and John Conlin and Peggy and
Eric Bardon, in the year of their fiftieth
wedding anniversaries

The publishers gratefully acknowledge the financial
assistance of Belfast City Council

First published in 1985 by
The Blackstaff Press Limited
3 Galway Park, Dundonald, Belfast BT16 0AN, Northern Ireland
and
51 Washington Street, Dover, New Hampshire 03820 USA

Typeset by The Brown Fox
Printed in Northern Ireland by
The Universities Press Limited
British Library Cataloguing in Publication Data
Bardon, Jonathan
    Belfast: 1000 years.
    1. Belfast (Northern Ireland)—History
  I. Title   II. Conlin, Stephen
  941.6'7   DA995.B5
Library of Congress Cataloging-in-Publication Data
Bardon, Jonathan, 1941—
    Belfast, 1000 years.
    Bibliography: p.
    Includes index.
    1. Belfast (Northern Ireland)—History.   2. Belfast
(Northern Ireland)—
History—Pictorial works.
I. Conlin, Stephen, 1959—   II. Title.
III. Title: Belfast, one thousand years.
DA995.B5B217   1985   941.6'7   85-22858
ISBN 0 85640 347 4

Introduction

In 1985 one of the exhibits attracting visitors to the Ulster Museum at Stranmillis, Belfast, is 'O'Neill's Chair', a curious stone seat rough-hewn from a single slab, displayed in an imaginative reconstruction of a room in a sixteenth-century Irish chieftain's castle. The chair is a permanent reminder that Belfast has a history centuries older than the town founded by Sir Arthur Chichester in 1603. In fact, this unique relic provides a link with a ritual rooted in pre-Christian times and once practised across the Indo-European world.

The chair was the installation seat of the Clandeboye O'Neills, and the ceremony in which it figured was described in ancient law books and later by English observers. The chief was inaugurated at a pagan site of remote antiquity: first he sat on the chair (in some other parts of Ireland it might have been a standing stone); then he was given a white rod symbolising his 'marriage' to his domain; and finally his principal vassal took off one of the chief's shoes and placed it on his own foot in recognition of his subservience. In his map of Dungannon, drawn at the end of the sixteenth century, Richard Bartlett pictured the inauguration chair of the Tyrone O'Neills at Tullahogue, but Fynes Moryson recorded in his *Itinerary*: 'In 1602 Lord Mountjoy brake downe the chaire wherein the Oneales were wont to be created, being of stone, planted in the open field.' The stone chair in the Ulster Museum is almost certainly the last of its kind surviving in the western world.

Early in the year of 1603 Conn MacNéill O'Neill, chief of Upper Clandeboye, had 'a grand debauch at Castlereagh with his brothers, his friends, and followers' in his stronghold on the site of what is now an Orange Hall, next to Lagan College in east Belfast. Soon all the wine in the castle was drunk and – William Montgomery recorded in the *Montgomery Manuscripts* – Conn sent his men . . .

> with runletts to bring wine from Belfast, unto the said Con, their master . . . they returning (without wine) to him battered and bled, complained that the soldiers had taken the wine, with the casks, from them by force . . . Con was vehemently moved to anger; reproached them bitterly; and, in rage, swore by his father, and by all his noble ancestors' souls, that none of them should ever serve him or his family, if they went not back forthwith, and did not avenge the affront done to him and themselves by those few Boddagh Sasonagh soldiers (as he termed them) . . .

Conn's servants returned to Belfast and attacked the English soldiers garrisoned there, killing one of them. More troops arrived, however, and 'the Teagues were beaten off and chased, some sore wounded, and others killed; only the best runners got away Scott free'. Conn O'Neill was found guilty of levying war against Queen Elizabeth and was thrown into a dungeon in Carrickfergus Castle. Though he was rescued shortly afterwards and was given a royal pardon, his power was broken and his lands were lost. The fall of Conn O'Neill marked the end of an era. Before 1603 had drawn to a close, Gaelic Ulster had been thoroughly conquered by the forces of the English Crown: Clandeboye was being colonised by the Montgomeries and Hamiltons; and Sir Arthur Chichester had begun building his town.

One hundred and fifty years later, when Belfast had become a flourishing port with 8,500 inhabitants, the ancient stone chair was found lying in the ruins of Conn O'Neill's castle. Stewart Banks, the Sovereign of Belfast, had the chair taken to the Butter Market at the lower end of Waring Street where it was built into the wall of the Weigh House. By the end of the eighteenth

century Belfast had a population of over 18,000 and had become the largest town in Ulster and the centre of Ireland's cotton industry. About this time the Weigh House was rebuilt and the stone chair was carried by one of the workmen, Thomas Fitzmorris, to his home in Lancaster Street where it attracted many visitors. By 1832 Belfast's population had leaped to close on 53,000, for the town was drawing in thousands of people from the impoverished Ulster countryside, in search of work in the steam-powered linen mills. In that year the stone chair was bought by a Mr R. C. Walker who took it to his estate of Rathcarrick in County Sligo. Sometime towards the end of the nineteenth century the chair returned to the north: by now Belfast, with a population of almost 350,000, was Ireland's largest urban centre and the fastest growing city in the United Kingdom. The chair was acquired for the Belfast Museum and Art Gallery in 1911, by public subscription. There, through the years of conflict and economic decline after the First World War, it attracted attention as a curiosity but its true importance remained unrecognised, until the new display was created in 1985.

The unveiling of this inauguration chair is but one example of the rapid growth of interest in Belfast's past. Since its new extension was opened in 1972, the Ulster Museum has drawn in visitors in ever increasing numbers to view the growing range of exhibits in the Antiquities and Local History departments. An equally impressive celebration of the past can be seen at the Ulster Folk and Transport Museum at Cultra. Local history societies are flourishing as never before: their journals and other local publications greatly increase our knowledge and interest. The recent history of Belfast has been characterised by violence, sectarian bitterness and mass unemployment: these troubles continue, but Belfast in 1985 shows more vigour than many would have thought possible ten years earlier. City-centre entertainments have enjoyed a remarkable revival and, to give but one popular example of a commitment to the future, Belfast Zoo is undergoing a thorough modernisation: animals are being moved from mean cramped cages and, perhaps most attractively, clean spacious quarters have been provided for a flock of Gentoo penguins and for the polar bear cubs Tumble and Wash.

This book does not attempt a general survey of Belfast's evolution – it is often difficult to visualise the past from outline histories. Instead artist and author have collaborated closely to open windows at fifteen successive stages over the last 1,000 years. Stephen Conlin has taken care to get close enough to show how earlier inhabitants of Belfast made a living, dressed and amused themselves. The book's unusually large format makes it possible for him to depict everyday life in lively detail, while at the same time giving a wide perspective to demonstrate how Belfast spread out from its historic core by the margins of the Farset stream. Belfast, even more than most Irish towns, has developed in response to political as well as economic pressure. For this reason each illustration has been linked to an event of national or international significance, and all but the first three are dated not only to a specific year but also to a particular day.

Stephen Conlin is firmly established as a talented artist and an inspired and meticulous draughtsman. In working on the illustrations in this book he has shown himself to be a painstaking and resourceful researcher – a vital quality, for there are no surviving pictures of medieval Belfast, and contemporary maps and representations are not abundant until the late eighteenth century. Annals, town records, travellers' descriptions, engravings and works of scholarship were consulted by the artist to ensure that his illustrations are as authentic as the surviving sources allow. Speculation has

been unavoidable, but it is speculation based firmly on archaeological and historical evidence. No record exists describing the castle at Belfast in 1489, for example: few scholars would quarrel, however, with Stephen Conlin's tower house, similar to contemporary castles in County Down.

Many people gave of their time most willingly in helping us to prepare this book. In particular we would like to express our gratitude to Tom E. McNeill, of the Queen's University Department of Archaeology, for his generous assistance and keen interest; Henry V. Bell, who lent much useful material and answered a stream of enquiries; Robert Bell, Gerry Healy, Heather Herron, Maureen Larmour, John Killen and Maureen Mackin, of the Linen Hall Library; Heather Grant and Roger Dixon, of Belfast Central Library; the staff of the Queen's University Library; Anne Millar, Noel Nesbitt, Richard Warner, Tom Wiley and W. A. Maguire, of the Ulster Museum; Emily Lee, Daniel Kerr and Barry White, of the *Belfast Telegraph*; Cynthia Wilson, Peadar Morris and Pat Brown, of the College of Business Studies; Betty Wilson and Ian Hill, of the Northern Ireland Tourist Board; Walter Williams, Grand Secretary of the Orange Order; Cecilia Coyle, of Richard Shops; Mark O'Neill, of Ulsterbus Ltd; Stephen Reid, of the Northern Ireland Fire Brigade; Douglas Carson; Robert McKinstry; Hazel McCance; Ciaran McKeown; David Livingstone; and Brian M. Walker. The illustrator wishes to express his particular thanks to David Gallagher and John Stewart. The author owes a debt of gratitude to Hilary Parker who edited the text with meticulous and sensitive care; to Barbara Fagan who not only typed the manuscript but also offered constructive criticism and support; and to Carol Bardon who compiled the index, read the proofs and gave much invaluable advice.

The inauguration chair of the Clandeboye O'Neills

1 The sandbank ford

In December 1947 workmen were busy levelling the steep-sloping ground at Shaneen Park off the Upper Cavehill Road. Their task was an urgent one for Belfast then was desperately short of houses: 56,000 dwellings had been destroyed or damaged in the Blitz of 1941, and many of the remainder were grimly overcrowded. A mechanical digger chugged steadily backwards and forwards, cutting into a low mound. Suddenly a deep hole opened up; the driver stopped his machine and called his workmates over. Peering in, they saw a great underground chamber lined with large stones carefully fitted together. The men were mystified by their discovery.

Estyn Evans, the distinguished archaeologist and geographer, lost no time in dashing up to the building site as soon as he heard the news. He not only identified the chamber as an ancient souterrain but also saw that it was sunk inside a rath, or fortified farmstead, much of which had already been stripped away by the mechanical digger. Unmarked on maps, this earthwork had become so overgrown that it had escaped the notice of generations of antiquarians and historians.

As soon as the weather permitted, Evans began the arduous task of excavation, with the help of a workman and some student volunteers. Innumerable fragments of pottery showed that this rath had been built some time in the tenth century – a thousand years ago this had been the defended home of a farming family on the slopes of the Cave Hill looking down on the river Lagan. Surrounded by a circular earthen wall and a stone-lined ditch, the *lios* or flattened enclosure was about 100 feet in diameter. Sherds of soot-stained pottery marked the position of several cooking fires; the pots, decorated by pinching or nicking with a finger nail, had steam holes characteristic of the period. Post holes and a few pieces of wattle and daub showed where a large dwelling had been erected in the centre of the enclosure. Lumps of slag lay where iron had been smelted and forged, and later a couple of tanged iron knives and some nails were discovered.

To take water out of the souterrain the team began to dig a deep trench only to find – once some rubbish had been shifted – that drains put there a thousand years before worked efficiently. Further investigation revealed that there were three chambers, connected and at an angle to each other, with corbelled walls curving inwards towards the top, and roofed over with huge slabs of rock. Descending by ladder from inside the rath, the inhabitants could seal the entrance and block up the connecting passage to take refuge in the innermost chamber. Evans established that the main purpose of the souterrain was to store food. Deep pits sunk into one chamber seem to have been for keeping milk, perhaps for making cheese and butter; wooden staves found here may well have been from a butter tub. Heaps of discarded bones demonstrated the importance of cattle in this economy – 85 per cent were ox, while only 14 per cent were pig and 1 per cent were goat, and there was also the leg-bone of a red deer.

No hoard of treasure trove was unearthed here to make headline news. The finds at Shaneen Park were modest enough – nothing more valuable than beads from a jet bracelet, a simple bronze cloak pin, a broken bronze buckle, a loom weight and a stone linen smoother. Yet the excavation had revealed much about the way of life on a self-sufficient farm a thousand years ago, where the city of Belfast now extends. More than twenty raths – today popularly known as ring forts – have been discovered just below the 600-foot contour line between the Cave Hill and the Black Mountain. Almost as many have been identified between the 400 and 500-foot contours on the Castlereagh and Holywood Hills. This was no wilderness: there had been

people here for the past 8,000 years and successive generations and incomers had felled most of the pine and birch trees on the hill tops, and levelled the forests of oak and elm in the lower Lagan valley. (Archaeologists' pollen counts confirm that there are more trees in Belfast and its vicinity today than there were a thousand years ago.) Hazel scrub and a scattering of poplar and ash marked the field boundaries. Close to the raths were carefully tended cultivation ridges growing corn, while cattle grazed in the outer fields. In summer flocks of sheep were taken up to the high pastures behind the Cave Hill and Divis Mountain. Here were standing stones, cairns and graves from a bygone age, raised by men who had first come to farm the hill tops 5,000 years before.

Below, in the Lagan valley, the ground was too heavy and waterlogged to be tilled by plough or spade. The river itself teemed with trout and salmon in season, and further upstream, amongst the reeds and thickets of alder and willow, otters, red deer and wild boar could be trapped and hunted. In Neolithic times the sea came up as far as Balmoral and the Lagan was forded at Ballynahatty in the vicinity of Shaw's Bridge. Near to this ford stand the remains of a passage tomb and an imposing enclosure, the Giant's Ring, a place of great ritual importance to the Neolithic farmers who had crossed here. In later Christian times, a thousand years ago, two churches – one at Shankill and the other at Knock – stood on dry ground on either side of an alternative crossing further downstream. Over the centuries mudflats had formed where the Lagan joined the sea and the estuary became broad and shallow; here, by a sand spit wedged between the Blackstaff and Farset streams where they joined the main river, the Lagan could be forded at low tide. The Irish named this *Béal Feirsde* (which means the mouth of, or approach to, the sandbank crossing), a name rubbed smooth by time to 'Belfast'.

The Celts who lived in and about the sandbank ford a thousand years ago may have shared a language but they were not a nation: warring dynasties fought over territory and sovereignty. The basic political unit in Ireland was the *tuath* (a word which survives in the English 'teutonic' and the German 'Deutsch'), a petty kingdom often no larger than a couple of townlands. The names of two of these are in everyday use in Belfast: Malone, *tuath Maoil Eóin*, 'the territory of the devotee of St John'; and Falls, *tuath na bhFál*, usually translated as the territory of the fences, but more likely it was 'Fál's territory'. These *tuatha* were dominated in turn by larger kingdoms. For centuries a people known as the Cruthin, subjects of the south Antrim state of Dál nAraidi, lived here, but their possession of the sandbank ford was often contested by the Ulaid of the east Down kingdom of Dál Fiatach. This is how Belfast got its first mention in history, for the *Annals of Tigernach* record in the year 666 'the battle of Fearsat', between the Ulaid and Cruthin, where Catharsach, son of Laircine, was slain'.

In 985 Vikings were raiding the north Antrim kingdom of Dál Riata. Would these Northmen turn south to ransack the Lagan valley as they had done in 933? For two centuries the Vikings had attacked these coasts again and again: the great monastery of Bangor had been burned several times and so often had longships penetrated up the Lagan that monks had built a round tower at Drumbo as a lookout and a refuge. The Northmen made camps at Larne and on the islands of Lough Neagh and no doubt the farmers above Belfast had often to seek refuge in their souterrains or in the caves, or make a desperate stand at McArt's Fort on the summit of the Cave Hill. Yet the invaders never conquered the land here and established only footholds in

Ulster. The raid of 985 came to grief, as the *Annals of Ulster* record: 'The Danes came on the coast of Dál Riata, i.e. in three ships, when seven score of them were hanged, and the others dispersed.'

Only a few place names in Ulster are of Viking origin, such as Strangford, the powerful inlet, and Carlingford, the inlet of the Viking leader. The overwhelming majority of place names in and around Belfast are Irish in origin. Identified meanings include: Stranmillis, the sweet stream; Shankill, the old church; Cromac, the bending – where the Blackstaff curved as it flowed into the Lagan, which itself means a river hollow; Ardoyne, Eoin's height; Divis, the black peak; Poleglass, the green hole; Ligoneil, O'Neill's hollow; Ballymacarrett, McArt's townland; Ballylesson, townland of the little fort; Gilnahirk, gillie of the horn, or hornblower; Knock, a hill; Ballynafeigh, townland of the fields; Cregagh, rocky place; Finaghy, white field; Galwally, territory of the foreigners; Ballygomartin, townland of Martin's enclosure; and Dunmurry, Muiredach's fort. A rath may have stood at the sandbank ford – the townland name for the spit of land between the Blackstaff and the Farset was Ballyrecoolgalgie, speculatively translated as 'the townland of the fort of Calgach's corner'.

The Irish in the north repelled the Vikings but their continued internecine strife was to leave them vulnerable in the following century to the next wave of marauders – the Normans.

Looking south-east from present-day Upper Cavehill Road

1 Rath earthwork
2 Dwelling house
3 Pot-making
4 Iron-smelting
5 Position of the sandbank ford on the Lagan river
6 Belfast Lough
7 Viking ships
8 Holywood Hills

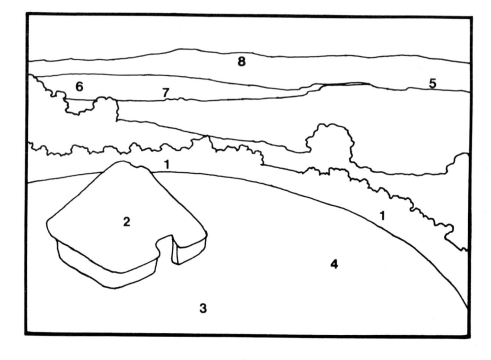

On Monday 24 June 1314 at Bannockburn, close to Stirling Castle, Robert Bruce won a great victory over the English and at last made good his claim to be the rightful king of Scotland. It was a battle which altered the destiny not only of Scotland but also of Ireland, a country which kept English armies supplied with both provisions and men. This neighbouring island King Robert meant to conquer, and it was to his brother Edward – brave in battle and steadfast throughout all the early years of failure – that he entrusted this great enterprise. Thus, while Robert carried the war into Northumberland, Edward Bruce gathered his veteran spearmen about him and struck a bargain with Thomas Dun, the renowned sea pirate, to bring together enough ships for the invasion of Ireland.

The English domain most immediately threatened was the Earldom of Ulster, which stretched from Coleraine to Dundrum. More than a hundred years earlier, these lands had been overrun by the Normans, who, from their many castles, kept the Irish in subjection. One such castle stood at Le Ford, the name the conquerors gave to the sandbank crossing of Belfast. A steep-sided 'motte', or mound, had been thrown up on the south bank of the Farset river and on its flat top a fortress had been built of heavy timber or stone. Protected by a circular ditch and a sturdy palisade, this castle stood sentinel over the river passage for the 'Red' Earl of Ulster, Richard de Burgo. Belfast was a borough town of the Earldom but the few humble dwellings clustered here made up no more than a hamlet, where the Earl's tenants sold their corn and cattle, paid their rents, or sought settlement of their disputes in the lord's court. Downstream, almost certainly on the site of the present St George's Church, stood the Chapel of Le Ford, one of several attached to the White Church at Shankill – the others were at Cromac, Stranmillis, Kilwee and 'Clochmestale', thought to have been on the road to Carrickfergus.

Above the castle the Farset had been dammed to give power to a water mill, and here farmers had their corn ground to flour: the profits from this mill amounted to 6s.8d. in 1326. There was a ready market for corn and much of it was shipped out to England from Carrickfergus, de Burgo's capital and the largest town in Ulster. On the Red Earl's demesne and on the de Mandeville manor in the lower Lagan valley the heavy clay soils had been brought under the plough, possibly for the first time, by the Normans. Most of the work, however, was done by the Irish who greatly outnumbered their overlords – this was disturbed country on the outer limits of territory controlled by the English crown, and few colonists could be induced to settle here. Defence of his lands was always the Red Earl's first concern and the castle at Le Ford was part of a network of fortifications around Belfast Lough, linking the mottes of Ballymaghan, Duneight, Knock, Dundonald and Holywood to the south with the massive stone keep of Carrickfergus to the north. Carrickfergus was to be vital to the survival of the Earldom as the Scots set sail.

On 26 May 1315, 300 vessels rounded the headlands of Islandmagee and steered into the shelter of Larne harbour. Never before had such an immense force of invaders come to these shores. This Scottish incursion was so unexpected that de Burgo was attending to his vast estates in the west 200 miles away, while Edmund le Botiller, the viceroy, was in Cork, 300 miles to the south. Edward Bruce led his 6,000 men inland, burning Dunadry and plundering manors in the valley of the Six Mile Water. Donal O'Neill, King of Tir Eoghain, crossed the river Bann to join the Scots and soon Edward Bruce was master of the north. One after another the castle garrisons – including that at Le Ford – capitulated. Only Carrickfergus held out.

At Carrickfergus Castle, after admitting settlers fleeing from the path of the invader, Henry de Thrapston wound down the portcullis and bolted the massive gates. As keeper of the castle and the Red Earl's treasurer, he trusted that the additional outer curtain wall and the new gatehouse would hold back the Scots. Anxiously he awaited the arrival of thirty crannocks of wheat he had ordered from Dublin: they never came, for the vessels were blown off course and the corn was sold in Carlisle by their commander, John fitzPhilip. The garrison, under the command of Sir Thomas de Mandeville, would have to survive on what lay within the castle storehouses.

Edward Bruce would not let Carrickfergus delay his conquest. Joined by the O'Neills, O'Hagans, MacGilmurrys and O'Cahans, he marched south, fighting his way through the Moyry Pass to Dundalk which he took and burned on 29 June. Meanwhile le Botiller advanced north with the feudal levy and was shortly joined by the Red Earl, leading a great host from Connacht. Seeing this, Edward Bruce slipped back into Ulster. Richard de Burgo demanded the honour of crushing the Scots, for not only had his Earldom been devastated but he felt betrayed: the Bruces were his kin – his daughter was King Robert's wife and his sister had married John the Steward, Edward Bruce's chief lieutenant. As the Red Earl pursued the Scots across eastern Ulster, both sides destroyed and plundered without mercy . . . 'Between them,' the *Annals of Connacht* recorded, 'they left neither wood nor lea nor crop nor stead nor barn nor church, but fired and burnt them all.' Then, on 10 September 1315, de Burgo was ambushed and routed at Connor near Antrim. His host scattered, the Red Earl fled south, leaving Edward Bruce supreme in the north. Only Carrickfergus remained defiant.

Meanwhile Ireland was gripped by famine. Constant rain had prevented the corn from ripening for several years in succession, and brought in its wake the most terrible dearth anyone could remember. Edward Bruce had planned to let his army live off the country, and now even his closest Irish allies had nothing to give. Once more he had gone raiding southwards but had been forced to pull back after many of the Scots had died of hunger and pestilence. Instead, Bruce drew his net tighter around Carrickfergus. There too the garrison was starving: in a desperate quest for food, Sir Thomas de Mandeville escaped from the fortress by sea and returned on Easter Eve 1316 with a flotilla of provisions ships from Drogheda. In the dead of night the vessels slipped past the Scots' ships guarding the mouth of Belfast Lough, and stole up to the castle. A vigilant Scot gave the alarm and all at once thirty of Bruce's men rushed down to resist the relief force: they fought until the last man, Neil Fleming, was slain. Members of the garrison made a desperate sortie from the walls, but it was too late. The whole Scots army was aroused, and, in furious fighting in the streets of Carrickfergus, Sir Thomas de Mandeville was killed. Grim hardships were to follow, for the corn never reached the castle.

In May 1316 at Dundalk Edward Bruce was crowned King of Ireland by his Irish allies. It was a title empty of meaning except in Ulster and even here the garrison in Carrickfergus refused to submit. Edmund le Botiller sent eight ships north from Drogheda in July with what little grain he could seize. Again, the corn never reached the besieged at Carrickfergus: the vessels were commandeered by the Red Earl and given to the Scots as ransom for his cousin, Sir William de Burgo. All hope for the beleaguered garrison disappeared. Every day men died of starvation, while the rest attempted to survive by chewing hides. The *Laud Annals* record that the garrison devoured eight captured Scots and explain that 'this pitiable circumstance' came about because 'no one came up with supplies'. Early in September 1316 Carrickfergus Castle surrendered.

In response to constant appeals from his brother, King Robert of Scotland sailed into Belfast Lough in December 1316, bringing fresh supplies and reinforcements. Together the brothers set out from Carrickfergus at the beginning of February 1317 and crossed the Lagan at Le Ford to start a long campaign southwards. Even though the Scots penetrated as far south as Limerick, the countryside they conquered was made worthless by famine and eventually it was starvation which drove the two kings back to Ulster. The dream of conquest was fading, and King Robert returned to urgent affairs in Scotland while King Edward Bruce lingered on to face defeat and death at Faughart, outside Dundalk, in October 1318. Even the Irish rejoiced at the slaying of Edward and the *Annals of Loch Cé* observed:

No better deed for the men of all Erinn was performed since the beginning of the world, for theft, and famine, and destruction of men occurred throughout Erinn during his time for the space of three years and a half, and people used actually to eat one another throughout Erinn.

Richard de Burgo recovered his Earldom of Ulster but the English colony there never fully got over the effects of the Bruce invasion. Less than a century later it would be the native Irish who would be guarding the river crossing at Le Ford.

Looking south-west from present-day High Street

1 The motte and castle of Belfast
2 The Farset river
3 The Chapel of the Ford
4 Sloblands
5 Robert Bruce accompanied by his squire and warhorse

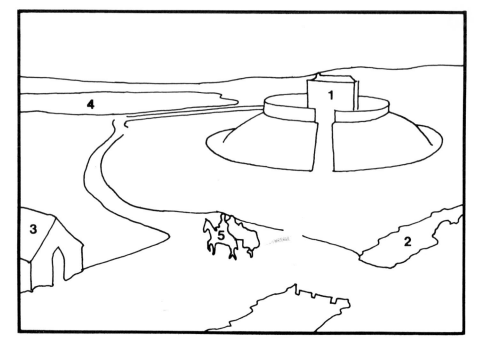

In the summer of 1489 Hugh Roe O'Donnell led a great host out of the woody fastness of Donegal. His leading kinsmen, wearing shirts of mail and mounted on agile ponies, looked fearsome as they raised their long spears above their heads. Behind them marched a column of warriors equipped with helmets and long mail shirts, and wielding two-handed battle axes. Each man was accompanied by an armour-bearer and a boy, for these were the MacSweeneys – O'Donnell's *gall-óglaigh*, or professional fighting men, of Hebridean origin, paid with oxen for every campaign. Joining this expedition were clansmen from townlands as far apart as Inishowen and Sligo, obeying the summons of their chief; they brought with them throwing spears, short bows, skeans and swords. These were O'Donnell's nimble skirmishers, or kern, and each man fought in his linen tunic, protected only by a round wooden shield and by his *glibb*, the tight bundle of hair at the back of the neck worn to cushion the force of a blow. Hugh Roe O'Donnell had been the undisputed lord of all Tir Conaill – a land never conquered by the foreigner – for twenty-eight years, ever since he had ousted and mutilated his predecessor, Turlough Cairbreach O'Donnell. He intended to take a great prey of cattle on this expedition by sweeping across Ulster, making the record of his *creagh*, or raid, a worthy entry in the *Annals of the Four Masters*, the O'Donnell chronicle kept by the O'Clery scholars.

At the other end of Ulster a castle stood at the sandbank crossing of Belfast. From here Niall Mór macCuinn O'Neill ruled Clandeboye, a sweep of territory encircling Belfast Lough from Whitehead to Bangor. These lands had fallen out of English control long since. The colony's disintegration can be dated from 6 June 1333, when the 'Brown' Earl of Ulster, the young William de Burgo, had been slain by his vassals at the ford of Belfast. The royal government had taken swift and merciless action against the murderers: '. . . all these foreigners fell in return', recorded the *Annals of Loch Cé*, 'having been either hanged, slain, or torn asunder by the king of the Saxons people'. But the victim had left no male heir and the divided Earldom was steadily overrun by the Irish. Emerging from the forests of Glenconkeyne, by the north-western shores of Lough Neagh, the *Clann Aodha Buidhe* (the family or descendants of Yellow Hugh, a thirteenth-century O'Neill king) had conquered the manors, granges and demesne lands in and about Le Ford. Only Carrickfergus, often garrisoned by fewer than a dozen men, remained independent of Clandeboye, the name the dispossessed English gave to this lordship of *Clann Aodha Buidhe*, which the Irish themselves named *Trian-Conghail*, Congal's third.

In 1489 the castle at Belfast would have been a tower house, similar to several erected about this time in County Down, such as Audley's Castle and Kilclief Castle. It would have been a tall keep, at least forty feet high, with two towers flanking the main entrance. The dimly lit ground floor was the storeroom, likely to have had a semicircular barrel-vault roof, temporarily supported by woven wicker mats until the mortar had set. The upper storeys would have been reached by a narrow winding staircase up one of the towers, lit by arrow slits. Food would have been cooked in braziers on the first floor and taken to the banqueting hall above. The uppermost storey would have been where the O'Neill chief slept under a gable roof, shingled with oak. Such castles had cells, built-in latrines, window seats, and secret chambers – in one Irish tower house the secret door could be opened only by sitting on a false latrine seat. The castle-dwellers' comfort in their cramped living space was sacrificed to defence, and sentries constantly patrolled the *bartizan*, or wall walk, behind the stepped battlements. The most striking feature of Ulster

tower houses was a bold arch connecting the two flanking towers; here there was a 'murder hole' for shooting at – or pouring boiling oil on – assailants attempting to ram the door below. Such a tower house could fend off local marauders, but it could not withstand a determined major attack. Belfast Castle had been taken in 1470 and 1476, when Niall Mór's father, Conn macAodha Buidhe, was lord of Clandeboye. It would be taken again in 1489.

Crossing the fords of the Foyle, Hugh Roe O'Donnell advanced through O'Cahan's country without opposition. Once over the Bann river, O'Donnell's army ravaged the MacQuillans of the Route and then swept southwards into Clandeboye towards the castle of Belfast. It is not known whether the castle fell by fire or assault, or if it was starved into submission – certainly it was destroyed, as the *Annals of the Four Masters* record:

> O'Donnell, i.e. Hugh Roe, the son of Niall the Rough, proceeded with an army into Trian-Conghail, in harvest time. He committed great depredations and devastations in the Route upon MacQuillan . . . He went from thence to Belfast, and took and demolished the castle of Belfast; and he then returned safe to his house, loaded with immense spoils.

Niall Mór O'Neill rebuilt Belfast Castle, but the task may not have been completed when Hugh Roe O'Donnell returned to raid Clandeboye in 1493. The annals record that Garrett Mór Fitzgerald, Earl of Kildare, destroyed the castle at Belfast in 1503 and took it again in 1512, the year of Niall Mór's death. The Earl was King Henry VII's chief governor of Ireland and these expeditions to Belfast were an early sign that English royal power would return to Ulster. However, it was not until 1573 that Clandeboye was seriously threatened.

In August of that year Walter Devereux, Earl of Essex, set out from Liverpool with letters patent from Queen Elizabeth granting him all of Clandeboye and much else besides. Arriving in Ulster with a formidable squadron, he soon decided that Belfast would make a more suitable centre for his colony than Carrickfergus:

> Belfast is a place meet for a corporate town, armed with all commodities, as a principal haven, wood and good ground, standing also upon a border, and a place of great importance for service, I think it convenient that a fortification be made there at the spring . . .

Essex seized Belfast and built a fort at Fortwilliam, but from then on his great enterprise began to founder. The Gaelic lord of Clandeboye, Sir Brian McPhelim O'Neill, constantly harried the settlers and on one occasion, Essex reported, the English 'were stayed at the ford of Belfast by the Rebels, who were gathered in great numbers upon the other side of the ford, to stop their passage'. Reluctantly Essex came to an agreement with Sir Brian, which included relinquishing the castle, but soon after he made up his mind to obtain by treachery what he could not win by conquest. In November 1574 he was invited by Sir Brian to a feast in Belfast Castle. The *Annals of the Four Masters* record the outcome:

> Peace, sociality, and friendship were established between Brian, the son of Felim Bacagh O'Neill, and the Earl of Essex and a feast was afterwards prepared by Brian, to which the Lord Justice and the chiefs of his people

were invited, and they passed three nights and days pleasantly and cheerfully. At the expiration of this time, however, as they were agreeably drinking and making merry, Brian, his brother, and his wife, were seized upon by the Earl, and all his people put unsparingly to the sword, men, women, youths, and maidens, in Brian's own presence. Brian was afterwards sent to Dublin, together with his wife and brother, where they were cut in quarters . . .

Instead of bringing him victory, this brutal action by the Earl of Essex aroused the whole of Clandeboye into furious rebellion. Very soon the Earl was forced to make a humiliating withdrawal from Ulster. He never abandoned his dream of returning and in a vain appeal to the Queen for help he wrote:

> I resolve not to build but at one place; namelie, at Belfast; and that of littel charge; a small towne there will keep the passage, relieve Knockfergus with wood, and horsemen being laid there shall command the plains of Clandeboye . . .

It would take more than one expedition to subdue Gaelic Ulster: only after nine years of gruelling warfare were the English able to build a corporate town at Belfast.

Looking south-west from present-day Castle Place

1 Belfast Castle of the Clandeboye O'Neills
2 The Farset river
3 Site of the motte castle
4 Hugh Roe O'Donnell and followers

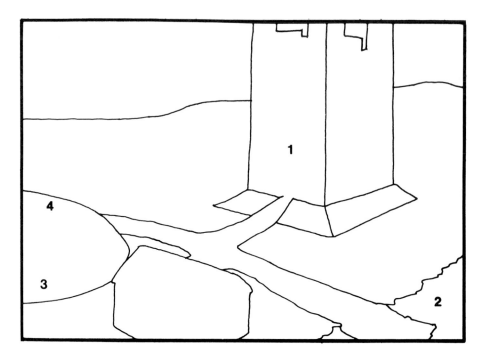

In the first years of the seventeenth century, as Queen Elizabeth's long reign was drawing to a close, Ulster was being ravaged from end to end. Hugh O'Neill, the Earl of Tyrone who once had two-thirds of Ireland at his feet, was now fighting a desperate rearguard campaign from the fastness of Glenconkeyne in mid-Ulster. Seizing cattle and burning cornfields, the forces of the Crown sought victory by starving O'Neill's people into submission. 'We have spoiled here good store of corn already,' Lord Mountjoy wrote from his camp by the Blackwater in 1601 . . . 'We mean to spoil it all, God willing, ere we go hence, and then cannot he keep any men this winter.' So terrible was the famine which followed, that parts of the province were described as 'desert' by the conquering English, and Fynes Moryson, Lord Mountjoy's secretary, saw 'multitudes of these poor people dead with their mouths all coloured green by eating nettles, docks, and all things they could rend up above ground'. On the Castlereagh Hills troops saw 'a most horrible spectacle of three children (whereof the eldest was not above ten years old) all eating and gnawing with their teeth the entrails of their dead mother, upon whose flesh they had fed 20 days past . . .'

In March 1603, six days after the death of the Queen, O'Neill's surrender brought the bloodletting mercifully to an end. Mountjoy's able lieutenant, Sir Arthur Chichester, had been responsible for the subjugation of eastern Ulster, and for his services to the Crown he was granted – in a patent dated 5 November 1603 – 'The Castle of Bealfaste or Belfast, with the Appurtenants and Hereditaments, Spiritual and Temporal, situate in the Lower Clandeboye'. Compared with other extensive lands he received in the province, the property at the sandbank crossing was, in Chichester's opinion, of little value . . .

> and albeit when I have it att best perfection I wyll gladly sell the whole landes for the wch others sell, five poundes in fee simple in these partes of the Kyngdome . . .

The successful planting of loyal Protestant subjects in Ulster, however, became the great passion of his life and so Chichester worked hard to set an example to his fellow countrymen by building a castle and a town at Belfast.

The Plantation Commissioners, reporting in 1611, were impressed by the progress made. Travelling eastwards from Sir James Hamilton's lands at Bangor and Holywood, they examined 'a stronge Forte buylte upon a passadge on the playnes of Moylon with a strong palisado and a drawbridge', where Shaw's Bridge now spans the Lagan.

> From thence we came to Bealfast where we founde many masons, bricklayers, and other laborers a worke who had taken down the Ruynes of the decayed Castle there almoste to the valte of the Sellers, and had likewise layde the foundacion of a bricke house 50 foote longe which is to be adjoyned to the sayd Castle by a Stayrcase of bricke wch is to be 14 foote square.

Surrounding the castle was a defensive wall 'almost finished which is flankered with foure halfe Bulworkes' and was 'to be compased aboute wth a lardge and deep ditche or moate wch will always stande full of water'. This was well fit to 'defend the Passage over the Foorde at Bealfast between the Upper and the Lower Clandeboye, and likewise the Bridge over the Ryver of Owenvarra

between Malon and Bealfast'. For the first time, a town of some importance was growing up at the sandbank crossing:

> The Towne of Bealfast is plotted out in a good forme, wherein are many famelyes of English, Scotish and some Manksmen already inhabitinge, of which some are artificers who have buylte good tymber houses wth chimneyes after the fashion of the English palle, and one Inn wth very good lodginges wch is a great comforte to the Travellers in those partes.
>
> Neere wch Towne the s^d Sr Arthur Chichester hath ready made above twelve hundred thousand of good brickes, whereof after finishinge of the said Castle, House, and Bawne, there wilbe a good proportion left for the buyldinge of other tenem^tes within the said Towne.

As James I's principal representative in Ireland, Chichester was instructed to ensure a Protestant majority in the Irish Parliament. This was achieved by 'incorporating' the new plantation towns, giving them the right to send members to the Irish House of Commons. In a charter dated 27 April 1613, Belfast became a corporation town: the borough was to be governed by a mayor or 'Sovereign', twelve burgesses and the 'Commonalty' or freemen of the town. In effect, the Corporation was composed entirely of Sir Arthur's nominees and it was he who selected Belfast's MPs. This monopoly of power would cause deep resentment in later times, but for the present Belfast prospered under Chichester's patronage.

Settlers brought more and more land into intensive cultivation and Sir William Brereton, a visitor passing through Belfast in 1635, found it 'a brave plantation' where colonists from Lancashire and Cheshire tended fields 'clothed with excellent corn'. In front of the castle gate, beside the Cornmarket, a Market House had been built. Favoured freemen of the town could set up stalls against its walls and were exempt from tolls. Outsiders had to pay dues levied by the Corporation: in 1635 these included 1d for a horse load or 'wheel car' load of goods; ½d for each load of timber or beasts driven through the town; and 4d for each animal slaughtered in the shambles.

The Town Book records many bye-laws to prevent the fouling of the river Farset and the 'Great Street', or High Street, flanking it on each side. The fine for throwing dye stuffs, carrion or 'any loathsome thing' into the stream was five shillings, and dunghills could not be left in front of street doors for longer than three days at a time. So much barley was malted for the brewing of beer that the kilns were a serious hazard, as a bye-law of 1638 makes clear:

> Fforasmuch as by dayly experience it is founde that mault kills erected in the body of this Towne are very dangerous and enormious and may upon the least accident indanger the whole Towne to be consumed by fyre, It is therefore Ordered and established by the Sovraigne & Burgesses assembled . . . That from henceforth noe p'son or p'sons inhabiting within the Burrough of Belfaste shall erect or make any mault kill, or make use of any mault kill already erected and built within the said Burrough, but in such convenient places as shalbe allowed of by the Lord of the Castle . . .

The forests of Dufferin and Killultagh were felled in a few short decades, and logs were floated down the river Lagan to Belfast, the best oak being cut by sawyers into ship timber and barrel staves for export to England. Most of the wood fed the charcoal furnaces at Old Forge and New Forge in Malone,

to smelt iron ore shipped in from Cumberland.

On 22 October 1641 Captain Lawson galloped hard from Killyleagh through Comber to his ironworks at New Forge. The native Irish of Ulster had risen and were advancing on Belfast from the west. Lawson found the citizens fleeing through the streets. He recalled:

> So I went throughout the town, and blamed them for offering to leave the town, and intreated for some arms, either by buying or lending, but could not prevail. At last I found in Master le Squire's house seven muskets and eight halberts, ready in the street to be shipped to Carrickfergus, which arms I took, and bought a drum, and beating the same through the town, raised about twenty men, who came with me again up to the Iron Works, having Mr Forbus, and some number with me, where also I gathered in all about 100 horse and foot.

Lawson's force reached Lisburn just in time to save the town falling to the insurgents. 'But for him we had Belfast,' Donal O'Kane remarked of Lawson, and in the respite thus won, the citizens of Belfast threw up a 'rampier', or rampart, to defend the five streets of their town. Besieged though it was in 1649, Belfast escaped the most devastating violence of these years of civil war. The town continued to grow and so much commerce passed through the three 'gates' of the rampier that by 1685 the cartographer Thomas Phillips believed Belfast was 'now the third place of trade in this Kingdom . . . having never less than 40 or 50 sail before it'.

Looking south-west from High Street

1 Belfast Castle, begun in 1611
2 The Farset river
3 High Street
4 Sir Arthur and Lady Chichester

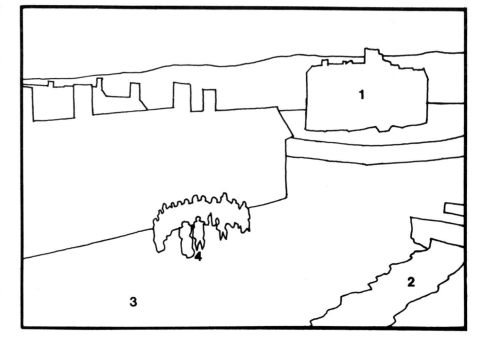

5 William of Orange in Belfast

On Friday 13 June 1690 the Duke of Schomberg rode into Belfast. For almost a year now this Huguenot general had been campaigning in Ireland, attempting with little success to wrest the country from King James and his French and Irish allies. Now his position was desperate, his horses without fodder, his Danish mercenaries without pay, and his troops decimated by scurvy and fever. He ordered men to all the nearby coasts and headlands to keep watch for King William's fleet: as the author of *An Exact Account of His Majesty's Progress* recorded . . .

We expect the King with impatience. The Castle of Belfast and the Castle of Hillsborough are prepared in the best manner to receive his Majesty. The streets of Belfast are daily swept, and not a horse permitted to go into any stable there, but all kept clean for the King and his Retinue.

Meanwhile William's fleet of about 300 vessels, escorted by Sir Cloudesley Shovel's squadron of warships, was having a difficult voyage. One officer wrote: 'The wind was very brave and the weather foggy, so that the Fleet often cast anchor to stop the tides and did not reach Ramsay Bay at the north end of the Isle of Man till ten of the clock on Friday night, being the 13th . . .' Soon after, the wind shifted and the Donaghadee post-boy galloped hard into Belfast to report that many ships were in sight – the Deliverer had come.

The best moorings had been taken by Schomberg's vessels so it was not until noon on Saturday that William's navy and supply ships dropped anchor. The King stepped ashore at Carrickfergus, mounted his horse and, as the author of *An Exact Account* records, 'rode through the main streets of the town, where almost numberless crowds received him with continued shouts and acclamations on till the Whitehouse . . .' It was at the White House, the home of Sir William Franklin at Macedon Point, that Schomberg met his King: Constantijn Huygens, a Dutch captain, noticed that William received the Duke coldly – perhaps because the general had achieved so little. The Prince of Orange accepted a seat in the Duke's coach; drawn by small Barbary horses and followed by another coach and a troop of horse, the King was taken along the shore to Belfast – the fastest route when the tide was out.

William entered the town by the North Gate about five o'clock. Never before had Belfast greeted so many men of distinction – Godert, Baron de Ginkel of Utrecht; Hans Willem Bentinck, the King's closest adviser; the Duke of Würtemburg-Neustadt, the German commander of the large Danish division; Count Henry Nassau; Prince Georg of Daamstadt, brother of Christian V of Denmark; the Duke of Ormonde, commander of the English Guards; the Duke of Manchester; and many others. The Rev. George Story, chaplain to one of William's regiments, recalled that the King . . .

was met without the Town by a great concourse of People who at first could do nothing but Stare, never having seen a King before in that part of the World, but after a while some of them began to Huzzah, the rest took it up (as Hounds follow a Scent), and followed the Coach through several Regiments of Foot that were drawn up in Town towards his Majesty's lodgings, and happy were they that could get a sight of him.

Another officer remembered that 'there were abundance to meet him at the North Gate, where he was received by the Sovereign and Burgesses in their formalities, a guard of the Foot Guards, and a general continued shout from thence to the Castle of – God Bless our Protestant King, God bless King William'.

Close to the North Gate William was met by the hero of the Siege of Derry, the Rev. George Walker, with twelve Anglican clergymen, who followed the coach to High Street and from there to the castle. Walker made a congratulatory speech and a verse address was presented to his Majesty. After urging William to 'Pull the stiff kneck of every Papist down', the poem continued:

Blest be the Angel brings the best of Kings
With expedition on the Cherub's wings,
Blest be the wind and tide that wafts you o'er
To your sad subjects on the Irish shore . . .

The King realised, with some alarm, that he was expected to make a speech; with considerable difficulty – for his English was very imperfect – this pale asthmatic monarch, his face lined with the constant pain of fighting ill-health, said that he had come to reduce Ireland 'to its due obedience, that his good subjects may not only be rescued from the present force and violence but be settled in a lasting peace, safety and prosperity putting his trust in Almighty God'. Afterwards, he relaxed by walking round the well-tended gardens of the castle.

The King remarked that he had not come to let the grass grow under his feet, and already his troops were coming ashore and unloading guns and supplies. The Huguenot soldier Gideon Bonnivert was impressed by Belfast, 'which is a large and pretty town, and all along the road you see an arm of the sea on your left, and on the right great high, rocky mountains, whose tops are often hidden by the clouds . . .' The author of *An Exact Account* was astonished by the size of the armada William had assembled before Belfast:

The Lough between this and Carrickfergus seems like a wood, there being no less than seven hundred sail of ships in it, mostly laden with provisions and ammunition . . . The great numbers of coaches, waggons, baggage horses and the like is almost incredible to be supplied from England, or any of the biggest nations of Europe. I cannot think that any army of Christendom hath the like. None but they that see it can believe it.

There were over forty pieces of artillery – six and twelve-pounder demi-culverins, nineteen and twenty-four-pounder cannon and mortars. Some of the Dutch guns required sixteen horses to pull them and altogether William had more than a thousand horses to draw his artillery and gun-equipment. King James II's spies reported back to Dublin that the Prince of Orange had £25,000 and several tons of tin halfpence and farthings: in fact William had brought £200,000 in cash to pay his men.

News of William's arrival spread rapidly. Camped out of sight of the town with a detachment of Schomberg's troops, Captain Sir Thomas Bellingham noted in his diary: 'A great shower of rain after dinner, about which time we fancied we heard some great guns off from Belfast which we hoped are for the King landing. Here came James Hunter, a Quaker, quartermaster of Levinson's dragoons. The King had landed . . .' Captain Rowland Davies, chaplain to Lord Cavendish's regiment of horse, galloped into Belfast, lit a bonfire and 'passed the night joyfully' with his fellow officers. Samuel

Mullenaux, an army physician, watched the celebrations in Belfast as darkness fell:

At night the streets were filled with bonefireworks which were no sooner lighted but the alarm signal was given by discharge of guns so planted that from one place to another of the army's several winter quarters throughout the whole country in our hands, in a few minutes, all places had been noted of the King's arrival, and in a very few hours, made bonefires so thick that the country seemed in a flame; so that the enemy could not but see the cause to their eternal grief.

Early next morning King William attended divine worship in the Parish Church in High Street but he was eager to engage King James without delay. On 19 June, after receiving a deputation of Presbyterian ministers and doubling their state salaries, he issued a proclamation to his troops to keep from pillage and injustice and rode out of Belfast. Stricken by a headache, he rested at Malone Grove; the delighted owner, Mr Eccles, renamed his house Orange Grove (later it was known as Cranmore).

On 30 June 1690 the Williamite navy was defeated at Beachy Head on the south English coast, but this was more than balanced the following day by William's victory at the Boyne. When the Jacobites capitulated a year later, Irish Catholics suffered severe religious restrictions and sweeping land confiscations. The Protestants of Belfast, however, were to benefit from their enthusiastic loyalty, and trade with the expanding British Empire brought them prosperity in the years to come.

Looking south-west from High Street
1 Belfast Castle surrounded by gardens
2 The Farset river
3 High Street
4 The Market House, offered to the Corporation in 1664
5 King William and the Duke of Schomberg received by the Corporation
6 King William's officers and commanders

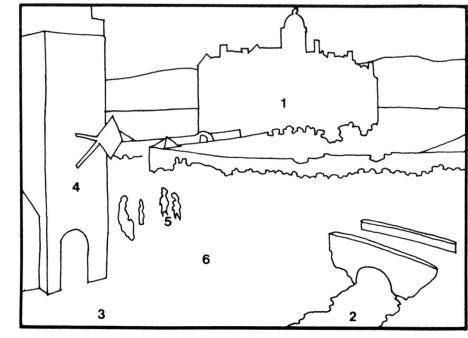

6 The *Sally* sails for America

FOR THE CITY OF PHILADELPHIA IN AMERICA

The good ship SALLY, burthen three hundred tuns, mounted with twelve carriage guns and six swivels, with small arms in proportion, Captain James Taylor, Commander, will be clear to sail from hence by the 15th day of April next for Philadelphia aforesaid . . . She is a fine new ship, and proves to be one of the fastest sailing vessels belonging to North America, and shall be amply provided with proper accommodations for passengers; and as the Captain is known to be well experienced in that trade, those who take their passage with him, may depend on the best usage. Dated at Belfast, March 1, 1762.

It was this advertisement which John Smilie of Greyabbey read in the *Belfast News-Letter*. Like so many Ulster Presbyterians, he saw America as a land of unbounded opportunity at a time when rents at home were rising fast; emigrants were promised plentiful cheap land where, in the words of a similar notice the previous year, 'they will be free of all tithes, and have their civil and religious liberties fully secured'. Despite the vigorous attempts of George Macartney, the Collector of the port of Belfast, to put an end to the emigration of the loyalist population, as many as 10,000 Protestants were leaving the province every year. The migration of Catholics across the Atlantic was not to begin for another century.

John Smilie bid farewell to his father on 18 May: he was in no danger of missing his ship, for the *Sally* was delayed, waiting no doubt for a full complement of passengers. Coming into Belfast by the road from Newtown Ards, he passed the country houses of squires and merchants, including Mount Pottinger. There, beyond the farmland and humble cabins of Ballymacarrett, was the Lagan mouth, spanned by the twenty-one arches of the Long Bridge, described by Edward Willis three years before as 'the longest in his Majesty's dominions'. Hawkers and pedlars did a brisk trade here and, that month, the stallion 'Tickle Me Quickly' stood at the County Down end, ready to cover mares at the cost of 'half a guinea, and a shilling'. Across the bridge, High Street was best reached from Ann Street by cutting through the lane by the old Parish Church. The castle, destroyed by fire in 1708, when three sisters of the 4th Earl of Donegall had been burned to death, stood no more at the top of High Street. No longer resident in Belfast, the Chichesters had neglected the town until recently. Now much of Belfast was being rebuilt and High Street was thronged with traders and dealers, while importers, shipping agents and sugar refiners in the entries were not short of customers.

Crossing the Farset by one of the High Street bridges, John Smilie walked to the New Street (later named Donegall Street) and there enquired for the house of Mr James Bashford; here Mr James Sinclaire, the agent, arranged his passage. The fare was generally around £5 and it is likely that Smilie became an 'indentured servant', agreeing to work without pay for a fixed term on an American plantation in return for a free passage. Taken by longboat from the dock, John Smilie boarded his vessel. On Monday 24 May the *Sally* weighed anchor, nosed past Carrickfergus and Whitehead and sailed northwards by the Antrim coast to steer west beyond Rathlin into the open Atlantic. 'Honoured father,' John Smilie wrote in a letter describing his voyage . . .

On the 31st we lost Sight of Ireland, having been detained 'till then by Calms and contrary Winds, which seemed to be the doleful Presages

of our after unhappy Voyage. We had our full Allowance of Bread and Water, only for the first Fortnight; then we were reduced to three Pints of Water per day, and three Pounds and a Half of Bread per week . . .

Grasping shipowners would keep food and water at a bare minimum, and unscrupulous masters would dole them out unfairly, but it was only when adverse weather delayed the voyage that passengers would starve. In 1729, 175 people had died on two Ulster vessels, and in 1741, forty-six died and six of their corpses were eaten by the surviving passengers when the *Seaflower* sprang her mast *en route* from Belfast to Philadelphia. During a fortnight of storms, the *Sally* was blown off course.

We had a South-West Wind, which drove us so far North, that our Weather became extremely cold, with much Rain and hard Gales of Wind: On the 5th of July we had a hard Squal of Wind which lasted 3 Hours, and caused us to lie to; on the 6th we had a Storm which continued 9 Hours, and obliged us to lie to under bare Poles; on the 12th we espied a Mountain of Ice of prodigious Size . . .

Britain was still at war with France and Spain, and Captain Taylor – disregarding the perilously low stock of food and water on board – eagerly pursued enemy merchant vessels in the hope of taking a prize:

. . . on the 16th we espied a Sail, which was along side of us before either saw the other; she having the wind right aft, crowded Sail, and bore away; we gave her Chase, and fired six Guns at her but the Fog soon hid her from us. In this manner did the Captain behave, giving Chace to all Ships he saw, whether they bore off us East or West . . .

The *Sally* was now ten weeks at sea and the ration was reduced to one and a half pounds of bread to last seven days. For the following twelve days each passenger attempted to survive on just two and a half biscuits, half a naggin of raw barley and twelve pints of water. Shortage of water made it impossible to eat the salt beef. As for the captain, 'neither he, nor his Mistress, nor five others that were his Favourites', were ever rationed:

Hunger and Thirst had now reduced our Crew to the last Extremity; nothing was now to be heard aboard our ship but the Cries of distressed children, and of their distressed Mothers, unable to relieve them. Our Ship was now truly a real Spectacle of Horror! Never a day passed without one or two of our Crew put over Board; many kill'd themselves by drinking Salt Water; and their own Urine was a common Drink; yet in the midst of all our Miseries, our Captain shewed not the least Remorse or Pity. We were now out of Hopes of ever seeing land. August 29th we had only one Pint of Water for each Person, which was all we passengers would have got, and our Bread was done; But on that Day the Lord was pleased to sent the Greatest Shower of Rain I ever saw, which was the Means of preserving our Lives . . .

It rained again, the winds were favourable, and on 1 September at 8 am they sighted land, 'to the inexpressible Joy of all our Ship's crew'. A few days later the *Sally* reached her destination, after a passage of fourteen weeks and five days in which sixty-four passengers died. Following a convalescence of three

weeks, John Smilie wrote to his father, who sent the letter to the *Belfast News-Letter* for the benefit of prospective emigrants.

Between 1750 and 1775 at least 143 emigrant ships left Belfast for America. The higher rents and fines imposed for the renewal of leases in Ulster – which encouraged many Protestants to endure the hardships of an Atlantic crossing – also fostered discontent at home. Angry farmers, calling themselves 'The Hearts of Steel', declared that 'betwixt landlords and rectors, the very marrow is screwed out of our bones . . . that the poor is turned black in the face, and the skin parched on their back'. On Sunday 23 December 1770 they surged into Belfast to secure the release of one of their leaders; they failed and soldiers firing from the Barrack killed five of them.

The 5th Earl of Donegall was blamed, with some justification, for causing this discontent. Under his patronage, however, Belfast made rapid progress in these years. New brick houses were built to strict standards. Lord Donegall presented the town with a handsome Exchange, completed at the 'Four Corners' (the present North Street/Bridge Street junction) in 1769, and the new St Anne's Parish Church erected in Donegall Street in 1776. Belfast, described by Lord Massereene in 1752 as being 'in a ruinous condition', had become, in the opinion of a visitor in 1783, a town which 'with some trifling improvements might be made to vie with any town in Ireland save Dublin and Cork'.

Looking south-west along High Street

1 Site of Belfast Castle, burnt down in 1708
2 The Farset river
3 High Street
4 The Market House
5 St George's Church
6 The *Sally* sets sail
7 Divis Mountain

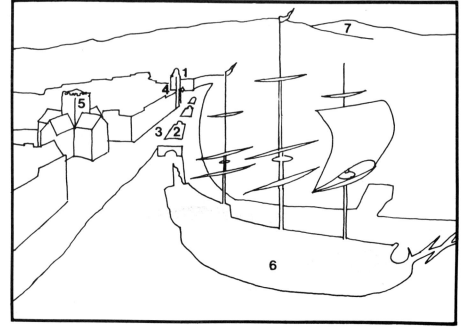

The lower Farset river was covered over in stages from 1770 onwards, making High Street the widest thoroughfare in Belfast. At the bottom of the street vessels tied up at high tide in the Town Dock and here, and at the adjacent Chichester Quay, firkins of butter, salt beef and salt pork, bales of bleached linens, and barrels of cured herring and salmon were hoisted aboard for export. Wines and brandies, raw sugar, exotic fruits, salt, coal, timber staves, iron ingots and other foreign imports were brought up from the dock on the backs of mules or in horse-drawn cars.

Close to the end of the eighteenth century Belfast had become a flourishing port with a population of around 19,000. The Joys and the McCrackens were typical of the Presbyterian merchant class which dominated the town's commercial and industrial life. Francis Joy had founded the town's first newspaper, the *Belfast News-Letter*, in 1737; so well did it prosper that it transferred from 'the Sign of the Peacock' in Bridge Street to larger premises on the corner of McKittrick's Entry and High Street. Joy's sons edited this news sheet and dammed the Blackstaff at Cromac to power their extensive paper mill; Henry led the consortium which built the White Linen Hall in Donegall Square in 1783, and Robert designed and promoted the building of the Poor House on the town's northern outskirts. Captain John McCracken lived next door to the Joys in High Street near Church Lane: shipowner, sailmaker, and proprietor of a rope-walk just north of Chichester Quay, he had the distinction of importing the first bale of raw cotton into Belfast. In 1778 he joined with his brothers-in-law, Thomas McCabe and Robert Joy, and built the town's first cotton mill in Francis Street at Smithfield. Twenty years later Belfast had become the centre of cotton manufacture in Ireland. Captain McCracken married Francis Joy's daughter, Ann; their third son, born in 1770, was Henry Joy McCracken.

The Joys and the McCrackens threw themselves enthusiastically into the Volunteer movement, founded in 1778 not only to defend Ireland from French invasion during the American War but also to campaign for Irish legislative independence and parliamentary reform. The Irish Parliament won the freedom to make its own laws in 1782, but the Presbyterians of Belfast deeply resented the Anglican Ascendancy's monopoly of power, so evident in their town where the two MPs and the members of the Corporation were the nominees of the 5th Earl of Donegall. The Presbyterians sympathised with the Catholics who sought emancipation from the remaining Penal Laws. St Mary's, Chapel Lane, Belfast's first Catholic church, was largely paid for by Protestants, and on its completion in 1784 the Volunteers paraded before it.

Presbyterian radicalism in Belfast was brought to a new pitch of excitement by news of the French Revolution. The Belfast celebration of the second anniversary of the fall of the Bastille was the most impressive in Ireland. In October 1791 the Society of United Irishmen was founded in Crown Entry, close to the Market House; its members were pledged to seek 'a complete and radical reform of the representation of the people in Ireland'. Henry Joy McCracken was amongst those who prepared to achieve democracy by armed insurrection. When the peasantry rose in furious rebellion in Leinster it was McCracken who, on 7 June 1798, led out the United Irish insurgents from Craigarogan rath to Antrim town.

By July 1798 Belfast was under martial law. Major-General Nugent had taken over the linen warehouses in Donegall Square South as his headquarters. The town was now the second largest garrison in Ireland and there were troops in all the streets: Fife Fencibles, 22nd Dragoons, York Fencibles, Argyle Fencibles, Monaghan militiamen, detachments of the Royal

Artillery, and cavalrymen of the local Yeomanry Corps. Belfast had been under the rule of the Army since March 1797 when General Lake, Nugent's predecessor – flogging, burning, and ransacking – had disarmed most of the United Irish conspirators. The result was that McCracken's 'Army of Ulster' was doomed to defeat. Nugent could congratulate himself that he had handled the difficult situation rather well and with a good deal less brutality than Lake in Wexford. Colonel Durham, Colonel Clavering and Lieut.-Colonel Ker had scattered McCracken's ill-armed men at Antrim town on 7 June 1798. Nugent himself, with Major-General Barber and Lieut.-Colonel Stewart, had then defeated a more formidable rebel army at Ballynahinch on 13 June. The French could send an invasion force at any time, however, and many of the leading insurgents were still at large – one of these was Henry Joy McCracken.

Meanwhile McCracken had come south from Slemish – where he had fled after the Battle of Antrim – through Glenwhirry and Ballyclare, in the hope of joining the insurgents in Down. From Divis he had seen smoke curl up from the cabins and cottages set alight by Nugent in Saintfield, and had heard the report of cannon fired at Ballynahinch. A messenger sent to Dunmurry had returned with news that the cause was lost. At the east side of the Cave Hill at David Bodle's cottage McCracken met his sister, Mary Ann; she gave him clothes, money, a forged pass and the promise of a passage on a foreign vessel moored in Belfast Lough. Disguised as a carpenter, carrying a set of tools, he set out from Greencastle for his ship. Crossing the Carrickfergus commons with two companions, he was stopped by four yeomen; one of them, a customer of the McCracken family, recognised the insurgent and refused a bribe, of a bond worth £30, not to betray him. McCracken was taken to Carrickfergus gaol and there visited by his father and sister. Mary Ann remembered: 'My mother had sent him a favourite book of his, "Young's Night Thoughts", and I observed a line from it written on the wall of his cell, – "A friend's worth all the hazard we can run." '

On Monday 16 July McCracken was brought under escort to the Donegall Arms Hotel in High Street, temporarily requisitioned as a gaol. Late in the afternoon, the prisoner was taken through Cornmarket and down Ann Street to be held in the old Artillery Barracks. Next day he was brought by Bridge Street to the Exchange, where six years before he had listened, fascinated, to performers at the Belfast Harp Festival. Mary Ann arrived as the trial was beginning:

> The moment I set my eyes on him I was struck with the extraordinary serenity and composure of his look. This was no time to think about such things, but yet I could not help gazing on him, it seemed to me that I had never seen him look so well, so full of healthful bloom, so free from the slightest trace of care or trouble, as at that moment, when he was perfectly aware of his approaching fate:

A verdict of guilty was certain. John Pollock, the Crown attorney, offered McCracken his life if he would name his co-conspirators. 'Harry, my dear, I know nothing of the business,' his aged father said, 'but you know best what you ought to do.' 'Farewell, father,' his son replied and whispered to Mary Ann: 'You must be prepared for my conviction.' Colonel Montgomery, the President of the Court Martial, condemned the prisoner to be hanged.

At the Artillery Barracks Mary Ann cut a lock from her brother's hair but Major Fox refused to allow her to keep it. Rev. Sinclair Kelburne, minister

of the 3rd Presbyterian Meeting House in Rosemary Street, arrived, and tears ran down his cheeks as he exclaimed: 'Oh, Harry, you did not know how much I loved you!' Together with Rev. Steele Dickson they prayed until it was time for the execution. Mary Ann remembered:

> About 5pm he was ordered to the place of execution, the old market-house, the ground of which had been given to the town by his great great grandfather. I took his arm, and we walked together to the place of execution . . . clasping my hands around him, (I did not weep till then), I said I could bear any thing but leaving him. Three times he kissed me, and entreated I would go; and looking round to recognize some friend to put me in charge of, he beckoned to a Mr Boyd, and said, 'He will take charge of you . . .'

John Smith recalled that 'the brave young fellow stood for a moment beneath the gallows, his eyes following the retreating figure of his devoted sister'. The family's standing in the town ensured a more dignified death for McCracken than for others executed as traitors at the time. The fly-blown heads of a Crumlin lawyer and two Ballynahinch insurgents already decorated a spike on the Market House.

Looking along High Street towards the Lagan river

1   The Market House
2   High Street (the Farset river was covered from 1770 onwards)
3   The Donegall Arms Hotel
4   Henry Joy McCracken (Mary Ann is led away by Mr Boyd.)

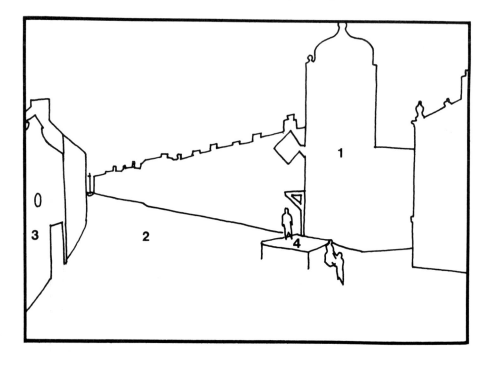

8 Rev. W.M. O'Hanlon walks among the poor

'After returning from some of these explorations,' the Rev. W. M. O'Hanlon wrote, 'and seating myself alone, I have really felt as though all were only an ugly dream – as if I had really been the victim of nightmare, and that a diseased fancy had conjured up all these loathsome and abominable things.' For the second time he had concluded a long letter to the editor of the *Northern Whig*, calling 'the earnest attention of the more affluent, respectable, and especially the Christian public of Belfast, to the deplorable condition of the poor who inhabit the back-streets, courts, and alleys, of our rapidly extending and populous town'. Appointed minister of the Congregationalist church in Upper Donegall Street in 1849, Rev. O'Hanlon was writing at a time when Belfast was experiencing unparalleled growth. Captain Gilbert, in his report of 1852 to the Lord Lieutenant, showed that Belfast had become the first port in Ireland, not only in the value of goods handled, but also in tonnage. The population of Belfast had risen from 19,000 in 1801 to 87,000 in 1851 and, as O'Hanlon pointed out, there were forty steam-powered linen mills in the city where twenty years before there had been only one. Yet behind the broad new streets and surrounding the mills were some of the most miserable scenes of abject poverty in Ireland.

The green fields between Donegall Street and the Poor House in Clifton Street had disappeared long since and had been filled with hurriedly-built and congested housing. Pushed by repeated potato crop failures and the collapse of the domestic linen industry west of the river Bann, the destitute had poured into Belfast. Eager to take work at the lowest wages in the thriving port and factories, the people of rural Ulster crowded into these narrow streets. 'I lay no claim to more compassion than my neighbours,' O'Hanlon wrote, 'but my soul has been sickened and oppressed, beyond the power of words to tell, by what I have seen . . .' In this letter, dated 15 September 1852, he described the area running from the Barrack in North Queen Street, through Carrick Hill and Millfield, to Smithfield:

Let me first direct your eye to some of the purlieus of North Queen-street. Every one must have noticed the close affinity existing between intemperance and the grosser forms of sensuality; and this quarter exhibits, in immediate juxtaposition, facilities for the indulgence of both these classes of vice . . .

Between Great George's Street and Frederick Street O'Hanlon counted twenty-two spirit shops and he found, staggering in and out of these, 'meagre, starving, squalid caricatures of men – aye, and of women too – mothers, with their naked infants in their arms . . .' O'Hanlon, however, did not blame alcohol for all the social ills of his day, as did many of his contemporaries. He quoted the celebrated words of Thomas Drummond, an Irish Under Secretary, that 'property has its duties as well as its rights'; condemning the slum landlords, he observed that 'the principle seems to be lost sight of in such squalid nooks'. He continued:

But, plunging into the alleys and entries of this neighbourhood, what indescribable scenes of poverty, filth and wretchedness everywhere meet the eye. Barrack-lane was surely built when it was imagined the world would soon prove too strait for the number of its inhabitants. About five or six feet is the space here allotted for the passage of the dwellers, and for the pure breath of heaven to find access to their miserable abodes. But, in truth, no pure breath of heaven ever enters here; it is

16

tainted and loaded by the most noisome, reeking feculence . . .

In an entry off Barrack-lane O'Hanlon found that seven out of nine houses were 'abodes of guilt' where counterfeiters, thieves and prostitutes 'all herd together in this place as in a common hell, and sounds of blasphemy, shouts of mad debauch, and cries of quarrel and blood, are frequently heard here through the livelong night, to the annoyance and terror of the neighbourhood'. Moving south to Carrick Hill, he observed twenty-one houses crammed into Campbell-court, and in Drummond's-court as many as three families living in each of its tiny four-roomed houses. Pepperhill-court was no better; here he saw that . . .

whiskey-drinking and lewd singing relieve the monotony of the scene, and the lazy and laden atmosphere is duly stirred at times by the frantic shouts of low bacchanalian orgies. It was from one of the doors in this vicinity that the fever-car had just departed on our arrival, bearing away to the hospital some wretched victim of miasma and foulness.

O'Hanlon could give no description of Stewart's-court 'because of the effluvium which met us on the very threshold'. He moved on to the courts and entries branching off North Street and there he wondered if citizens other than rent collectors ever saw the 'spectres of want and destitution that tenant these neglected and unknown receptacles of the lowest grade of our population'. Round-entry harboured 'the most loathsome corruptions'; in McTier's-court he saw that the main business was stone-breaking which 'yields but a miserable subsistence'; and in Peel's-court he counted 'twelve families in six houses, and shut in – narrow and close – between two nuisance-yards, one for the front and another for the back, where the air is such that we could not stand a moment without a sense of deadly sickness and loathing warning us to flee from the foul spot'. In Millfield O'Hanlon encountered 'wan mothers, and sickly, emaciated children all around'; he predicted that cholera would return to Belfast and 'that, by a righteous retribution, the population of our sumptuous streets and handsome town houses will be made to pay the penalty of neglecting the sanitary and social condition of their less fortunate fellow-townsmen'. In 1854 this 'fearful pestilence' did 'again come westward with deadly step' and 1,087 cases and 563 deaths were recorded.

In the same month as O'Hanlon wrote this letter, September 1852, Dr Andrew Malcolm read a paper before The British Association entitled, 'The Sanitary State of Belfast'. Historian of the General Hospital in Frederick Street and a tireless campaigner for improved public health, he gave statistical proof of the close connection between filth and fever. 'Certain it is,' he observed, 'that, in several spots, the germs of fever have remained unmoved, nay I might say unmolested, for a period of thirty years.' He calculated that over those past thirty years fever had attacked 62,000 citizens of Belfast, of whom 6,000 perished. Spacious and well-drained suburbs had only been lightly affected but the congested districts surveyed by O'Hanlon had the highest incidence of fever, especially in the terrible epidemic of 1847: Drummond's-court, with only forty-one houses, had 113 cases between 1837 and 1847; the Old Lodge Road 166 cases; and Pinkerton's Row 295 cases. Outbreaks of fever and cholera were closely associated with 'deficient drainage, want of house accommodation and pure air without, and want of room and cleanliness within'. Even without fever, the death rate in the Dock and Smithfield districts

was as high as anywhere in the United Kingdom. In these squalid slums children were particularly vulnerable: Dr Malcolm calculated that in 1852 – a year without famine or cholera epidemics – the average age of death in Belfast was nine years, because the 'infant mortality is absolutely excessive'.

A major cause of this deprivation, not discussed by Dr Malcolm, was that the making of linen had become the principal source of employment in Belfast. Wages were lower than in any other textile factories in the United Kingdom – as late as 1885 spinners earned 8s. 5d. and preparers 6s. 10d. a week. The usual working day began at 5 am and ended at 7 or 8 pm with only two half-hour breaks. Mill-hands had therefore to live close to their work and could afford only the meanest rented rooms. Severe accidents from unprotected machinery were frequent. Dr John Moore, writing in 1867, observed that machine boys were often 'under my care for wounds and laceration . . . generally of the most frightful character, and fatal in their results'. He believed that, nevertheless, linen manufacture was 'one of the most healthy in the whole range of our manufactures'. It was left to Dr C. D. Purdon in the 1870s to describe the terrible effect of flax dust on the health of linen workers, giving them attacks ending 'in vomiting or in expectorating a glairy mucus' and severely shortening their lives.

Drawn to Belfast by the growing prosperity of linen, the rural poor settled in very distinct districts such as the Protestant Sandy Row and Shankill and the Catholic Markets and Short Strand. It was on the frontiers of the most sharply segregated enclaves that bitter sectarian fighting was to flare up in the years to come.

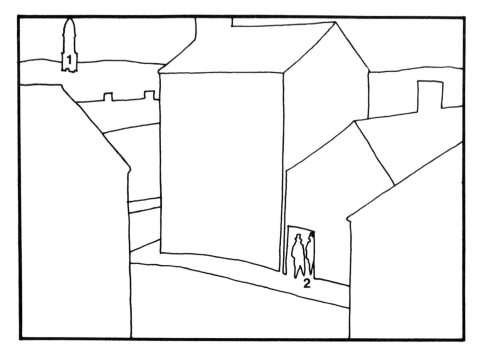

Looking south from the area between North Queen Street and York Street

1 The tower and cupola of St Anne's Church, Donegall Street, demolished in 1900
2 Rev. W. M. O'Hanlon and companion

9 The funeral of John McConnell

Thursday
18 August 1864

At first light on Tuesday 16 August 1864 angry crowds were already gathering at the street corners in Sandy Row and the Shankill, and in the Catholic district wedged between them, the Pound. By 5 am a furious battle raged in Brown Square on the Shankill; seven were injured by gunfire and one man fell mortally wounded. When the first train from Dublin drew into the Great Victoria Street terminus, a mob from Sandy Row attacked the passengers as they alighted. Alerted by one of his constables, John Caulfield, an Irish Constabulary sub-inspector, led out his men from the Albert Crescent barracks into Durham Street. Sent up from Co. Meath only the previous Friday, Caulfield was now faced by people from Sandy Row ferociously determined to press home their attack on the Pound. Three times waves of attackers pelted his force with cobblestones and shots were fired by the rioters during the last wave. Struck on the chest by a spent bullet, Caulfield raised his Constabulary sword with its serrated edge and ordered his men to take aim. Amongst those who fell in the volley was John McConnell; wounded in the skull, he died shortly afterwards in the Union Workhouse hospital on the Lisburn Road. In his *History of the Belfast Riots*, written a few weeks later, Thomas Henry declared that 'the memory of the sub-inspector who was guilty of this unmanly outrage will long be detested by the Protestants of Ulster'.

In the opinion of historian/journalist F. Frankfort Moore, the riots, which had convulsed much of Belfast for eight days in succession, were caused by . . .

the importation the previous year of some hundreds – perhaps thousands – of navvies to build a new dock, and it was found out that a large proportion of these men were Roman Catholics. The balance of the fighting power among the belligerent classes was thereby disturbed; so when the illegal "walking" of the Protestants on the Twelfth of July was interfered with by the opposite party, the result was a series of encounters in many of the streets. It was, however, only when the Romanists tried to organize a party procession of their own later that the town was given over to civil war . . .

In peaceful times sixty-five members of the Irish Constabulary were stationed in Belfast in addition to 160 Town Police under the command of Chief Constable James McKittrick and his deputy, Thomas Green. After Catholic navvies had rampaged through the town centre and made a savage attack on Brown Square National School on Monday 15 August 1864, Dublin Castle sent up a special train of twenty-seven wagons carrying two field guns and substantial reinforcements of constabulary, cavalry and infantry. On Wednesday 17 August Protestant shipwrights made a concerted and devastating attack on the navvies at work at the new docks; one was killed and many received terrible wounds.

Thursday 18 August began calmly enough, the *Northern Whig* reported: 'Immense crowds assembled at the various corners armed with every conceivable weapon, but in every street the great force of police and military prevented the continuance of mob law.' Breaking off a holiday in Harrogate, the Mayor of Belfast, John Lytle, returned that morning and attempted in vain to prevent loyalists from turning John McConnell's funeral into a massive display of Protestant strength. The local magistrate, William Lyons JP, set aside military advice to ban the procession which was expected to travel the two miles from Sandy Row to the Knock burying-ground by a

18

direct route along Howard Street and May Street, across the Queen's Bridge and through Ballymacarrett. Unknown to the authorities, however, the organisers were preparing to skirt menacingly past the Pound and the Catholic butchers of Hercules Street.

Shortly after 3 pm the hearse set out from Sandy Row, followed by thirty cabs and jaunting cars, and at least 5,000 men marching four and six abreast. Lyons, accompanying the funeral, was caught unprepared when the procession turned into Wellington Place. When, opposite the front gates of the White Linen Hall, the hearse halted, Deputy Chief-Constable Green later recalled that he ordered the driver to go straight on into Chichester Street: 'I saw him giving way to the funeral party to take Donegall-place, and I seized one of the horses by the reins; immediately a large party of people got at the other sides of the horses and shoved them round, and the funeral afterwards took Donegall-place.' As the hearse turned into Belfast's most fashionable street there was a roar of approval from the loyalists who now openly brandished arms – including fearsome bludgeons studded with nails, and scimitars fashioned from barrel hoops – and, as James Kennedy JP recalled, 'I saw pistols with the men. I think every man had a pistol.' Meanwhile District-Inspector McCarthy and a few constables were desperately attempting to hold back armed Catholics massing in Hercules Street. A shot was heard and then, the *Northern Whig* reported, 'from along the line of the procession in the funeral, volley after volley was fired. On coming nearer Hercules Place, the gunshots got more and more numerous.' The *Belfast News-Letter* continued:

When the funeral procession reached the head of Donegall Place a mob of butchers and navvies, armed with pistols, cleavers, and other formidable weapons, had turned out of Hercules Place into Castle Place. They fired a shot, then another, and then they cheered, apparently by way of challenge of fight . . . just as two men advanced up the street and fired again towards the *cortege*, which kept on its steady solemn pace.

In vain army officers attempted to persuade Lyons to use the force at his disposal to turn the funeral around. He said later in evidence: 'I will tell you what struck my mind after the firing began – "D—n me, but here I am with the Queen's Hussars attending an illegal procession, and what am I to do?"' It looked as if he was leading the procession. The *Northern Whig* described the scene in Castle Place:

On the appearance of the Hussars, a tremendous cheer was raised by the funeral party, and orange handkerchiefs were waved in great numbers. Whilst this scene was going on, we observed a man who had been closely following the hearse, and who, from wearing crape, was probably a relative of the deceased, taking out a rifled pistol of large size and firing shots rapidly and continuously, as fast as he could reload, in the direction of Hercules Place corner. The guns fired continuously, the bullets pierced the air, whirr after whirr, in a continuous volley . . .

Shots were fired into the home of Bernard Hughes, owner of a bakery and the leading Catholic layman in Belfast. Windows were broken, an officer's hat was shot off and several men were wounded; no deaths, however, were recorded. Led on by Lyons and the Hussars, the procession got through High

Street and across the Queen's Bridge, with the Dragoons bringing up the rear. While the hearse passed Ballymacarrett Parish Church, clergy produced orange sashes. After the funeral, the procession returned from Knock by Chichester Street, cheering the unhappy Mr Lyons outside the White Linen Hall.

That evening about 100 houses were wrecked in Stanhope Street and off the Lodge Road. A Presbyterian minister, the Rev. Isaac Nelson, made this submission to the Belfast Inquiry Commission:

The mobs in my neighbourhood not only hunted poor Roman Catholic neighbours out of their houses, but I had to go and beseech them to grant so many hours to these poor people to take their furniture out . . . I could have sat down and wept when a poor little girl came with a pet canary bird in a cage, when the poor people had been driven from their houses, the children in one direction and the father and mother in another . . .

By Thursday night there were almost 1,000 men of the Irish Constabulary, 150 Town Police, 600 special constables, six troops of the 4th Hussars, infantry of the 84th Regiment, and half a battery of artillery in Belfast. This great force, together with what Frankfort Moore called 'the usual autumn monsoon' brought the 1864 riots to an end.

Looking north-west from Castle Place (same viewpoint as page 31)

1 Castle Place, leading to High Street
2 Hercules Place, demolished in 1879-81 to make way for Royal Avenue
3 The Bank Buildings
4 The Ulster Club, built in 1861 and demolished in 1981 to make way for
      new Post Office building
5 Clifton House
6 Cave Hill
7 Catholic crowd
8 Protestants following the hearse of John McConnell

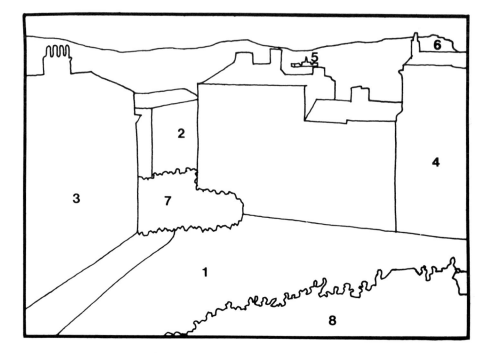

From early morning special excursion trains drew in at the Great Northern, Belfast & County Down, and Northern Counties railway stations bringing sightseers from all over Ulster to view the launch of the *Oceanic*, the largest ship in the world. According to the *Belfast News-Letter*, there were also visitors 'from London, Liverpool, Glasgow and all other great British ports, from the United States – whose people venerate enterprise and esteem affectionately everything which is big – and from almost every European country'.

The weather was bright and sharp as immense crowds made their way to the riverside. A large pavilion had been put up on Victoria wharf, providing seating for 2,000 and a promenade for another 3,000. On the Queen's Road men of the Royal Irish Constabulary and a detachment of the North Staffords Regiment held back the throng as people of rank and fashion drove up in their carriages. Far greater numbers crowded on the Antrim shore where a barrier had been erected to prevent the unwary being pushed into the river, and a force of 'bulkies' – the Harbour Police – manned the Milewater Bridge. Here a *Belfast Telegraph* reporter mingled with the closely packed onlookers. He listened to a conversation between two men hoping to see an exciting disaster: '"We shan't be disappointed today, William," said Andrew. "There can't be a mistake today, someone is bound to be hurt," William replied.' Another correspondent of the same newspaper watched from aboard a tug; close by, on the barque *Romanoff*, moored near the entrance to Prince's Dock, he saw about two dozen men on the top gallant spars, 'and most singular of all, several grey-haired veterans, who were willing to remain for quite an hour in such a dangerous and exposed position'.

All eyes faced the huge gantry on Queen's Island where 17,000 steel plates had been affixed by 1,704,000 rivets to nine-inch frames of channel steel and five steel decks, to create the *Oceanic*. From modest beginnings on an island of mud cast up by the dredging of the Victoria Channel, the Harland & Wolff yard had grown from one and a half acres employing 100 men in 1854 to eighty acres and 10,000 men by 1899, making it the most extensive in the world. Shortly before, a correspondent of the *Windsor Magazine* had described work in progress on the Island:

> Men rush about with great plates of steel on handcarts; there is the creaking of cranes as the plates are swung through the air into place, the clang of hammers reverberating again and again. Every vessel is surrounded by a network of scaffolding, and inclined wooden ways are built to the top of the ship. Chains, pieces of iron, heaps of bolts and blocks of wood litter the ground, and you shudder as the casual remark is made to keep out of the way of falling bolts . . . on the average a baker's dozen of men are killed in the course of a year . . .

The *Oceanic* was the second ship of that name built by Harland & Wolff for the White Star Line of Liverpool. All the White Star liners had been constructed by Harland & Wolff and now that line urgently needed a competitor to rival North German Lloyd's *Kaiser Wilhelm der Grosse* and Cunard's *Campania* and *Lucania* in the lucrative transatlantic passenger market. With a gross tonnage of 17,274, a length of 685.7 feet, a breadth of 68.3 feet, a hold of 44.5 feet, and fitted with four-cylinder triple-expansion engines, the *Oceanic* would outdistance all rivals: thirteen feet longer and eight feet deeper than Brunel's *Great Eastern*, she would be the largest ship afloat and the longest ever launched.

The crowds were 'very patient and good-humoured', the *Belfast News-Letter* observed: 'Of course, some of the old war cries were trotted out and bandied about freely, an antiphonal chorus of "Go on the blues" being the principal feature of this method of beguiling the time.' As the launch became imminent, the *Belfast Telegraph* noticed that . . .

> a dead silence of suppressed excitement permeated the people on the shore and on the top. A rocket went up, and the people asked in low tones: 'Is she moving?' No she did not move! Then there was another loud report. 'There's another rocket gone!' exclaimed the multitude. And they stared with every optical nerve strained at the leviathan. No movement yet! The excitement became deeper! Then a man said in an awestricken voice: 'Isn't it like an execution?' . . .

The first rockets signalled the arrival of distinguished visitors at the pavilion, including the White Star chairman, Thomas H. Ismay; Gustav Wolff MP; the Duke and Duchess of Abercorn; the Marquis and Marchioness of Dufferin and Ava; the Earl of Shaftesbury; the Marquis of Hertford; and Colonel Edward Saunderson MP, the Ulster Unionist leader. 'Bad for weak action of the heart this,' a man said as a rocket made another loud report to warn off tugs scudding about inquisitively near the ways. Two guns were fired to signal the shipwrights to stand aside, then Harland & Wolff's general manager, Mr A. M. Carlisle, waved the launch flag, and – released by a hydraulic trigger – at twenty-seven minutes past eleven the *Oceanic* began to move. As the great vessel slid down, the *Freeman's Journal* reported, 'Pieces of timber as large almost as forest trees rose into the air like chips in a wind and fell in showers on the water. Presently the great hawsers, which held the two immense bow chains in sections began to break and fly into the air . . .' Six chains, with links each two feet long and weighing half a hundredweight apiece, held the vessel; length after length of cable ran out, with the restraining rope stoppers snapping sharply as they yielded to the immense strain put on them. Then, the *Belfast News-Letter* continued:

> The occupants of the stands jumped to their feet, the small army of photographers began their deadly work, and a tremendous cheer went up from the assembled thousands on each side of the river. Like a gull alighting with graceful curve on the water came the *Oceanic* from the ways, her beautiful lines showing to magnificent advantage as she settled with an accompanying displacement of the placid waters of the river . . .

The chains, anchors, and stops pulled up the liner within a little more than her length. Sirens, foghorns, and steam whistles continued for some time after the cheering had died away. The displacement wave showered the closest spectators 'and the merriment was increased as the wave, washing underneath the wharf, caused the dirt and dust in the interstices of the planks to shoot up, to the further confusion and discomfort of the unlucky ones'. '"Never mind," William said in disappointment to Andrew, "better luck next time."' The *Freeman's Journal*, often scathing about Belfast's pretensions, described the launch as 'the greatest event of its kind the world has ever witnessed, and in a certain sense, perhaps the most epoch-making incident of the century'.

A wide range of attractions awaited visitors who had attended the launch and wanted to complete their day. That evening at 7.30 there was a 'Cinematograph Display' of the launch 'on the windows' of the *Belfast Telegraph* offices in Royal Avenue. At the Theatre Royal in Castle Lane F. R. Benson's Shakespearean Company was putting on its last performance of *Romeo and Juliet*. The Christmas pantomime *Babes in the Wood* was still showing in the Grand Opera House, completed to Frank Matcham's lavish design three years earlier. Seats in the Alhambra Theatre of Varieties in North Street could be had for as little as sixpence to see The Great Friscari, The Three Gesters, and the Marvellous Zoës. George Beauchamp could be seen at the Empire Theatre of Varieties in Victoria Square, rebuilt in a Moorish style five years before. At the corner of Donegall Street and Royal Avenue, the Great Menagerie & Circus of Varieties might have been worth a visit, and some children would have been allowed to stay up to watch the animals being fed at 9.30 pm. At Carter's Waxworks & Wonderland, 10 Ashe Place, the management proudly presented the Electric Lady, La Forge Mephisto: 'Electric sparks will fly from the young lady's limbs almost as profusely as from a blacksmith's anvil when forging red hot metal.'

These were the entertainments of a great city which had recently bypassed Dublin to become the largest in Ireland. The prosperity of shipbuilding, engineering and linen manufacture continued to draw in thousands from the surrounding countryside so that, by 1901, only one in five of Belfast's householders had been born in the city. The Town Hall in Victoria Street was no longer a fitting municipal centre: the White Linen Hall in Donegall Square had been levelled and H. & J. Martin were about to begin the construction of the City Hall.

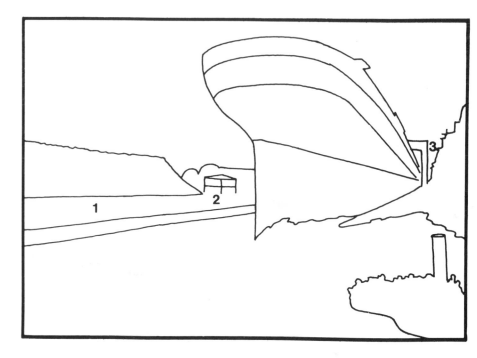

Looking south-east towards Queen's Island

1 Victoria Wharf
2 Queen's Island
3 The gantry

11 Signing the Covenant

Ulster Day dawned bright and clear, and defied the forecast by remaining almost cloudless. 'There was a Sabbatical appearance about the streets in the early morning,' the *Belfast News-Letter* observed:

The clang of the hammer, the throbbing of machinery, and the whirr of the loom were no longer heard, and the artisans, dressed in their best attire, joined their employers in the services at the various Churches, where Providence was supplicated to avert the very grave and real danger that threatens the country . . .

The danger to Protestant Ulster was that the Liberal government's Third Home Rule Bill was about to pass the Commons, and by the terms of the 1911 Parliament Act, the Lords could delay but not kill this limited measure of self-government within the Empire. Ulster Unionist leaders believed that only a massive display of unflinching resolve could halt this threat to Protestant liberties. Vicious sectarian rioting had been the response to the Home Rule Bills of 1886 and 1893. Already in July 1912 some Catholic workers had been driven from the shipyards and as recently as 14 September a bitter conflict had disrupted a football match between Linfield and Celtic. The loyalist protest must, it was felt, be disciplined and not sullied by violence which might alienate British public opinion.

At 9.15 am on 28 September a guard of 2,500 men recruited from the Unionist Clubs of Belfast gathered at the City Hall; at 10 am the first relief of 500 men wearing bowler hats and white armlets, and carrying white staves, began the daylong task of marshalling the crowds and protecting the flowerbeds. The Portland stone of the City Hall gleamed in the sun: formally opened six years before, this was one of the most sumptuous municipal centres in the United Kingdom, a fitting pivot of the resistance to Home Rule. Belfast was the very heart of loyalist Ulster: three-quarters of its 387,000 citizens were Protestant and almost all of its business and trade was in Protestant hands. Belfast was one of the great cities of the British Empire: it had the world's largest shipyard, ropeworks, tobacco factory, linen spinning mill, tea machinery works, aerated water factory, and dry dock; Harland & Wolff had launched the world's biggest ships – the *Olympic* in 1910 and the *Titanic* in 1911. To most of its citizens Belfast's prosperity depended on its remaining an integral part of the Empire. Now they prepared to give fervent expression to the strength of their feeling.

Just before 11 am Bedford Street was packed with spectators as Sir Edward Carson, the Dublin lawyer who led the Ulster Unionists, stepped into the Ulster Hall. As he took his place on the platform, behind which was displayed the largest Union Jack ever woven, Sir James Craig reminded everyone in the packed hall that there should be no applause as this was a religious service. The congregation sang 'O God, our help in ages past', and after prayers and lessons had been read the Rev. Dr William McKean rose to deliver his sermon, taking as his text Timothy 6.20: 'Keep that which is committed to thy trust.' 'We are plain, blunt men who love peace and industry,' the former Presbyterian Moderator declared: 'The Irish question is at bottom a war against Protestantism; it is an attempt to establish a Roman Catholic ascendancy in Ireland to begin the disintegration of the Empire by securing a second parliament in Dublin . . .' All over Belfast similar services were being held in Protestant churches.

From the Ulster Hall Sir Edward walked bareheaded into Bedford Street towards Donegall Square. Captain Anketell Moutray Read proudly carried

22

before him King William's flag, a yellow banner decorated with a star and a red cross, said to have been borne at the Boyne. The guard of honour which had escorted Carson – splendid with military medals, specially embroidered sashes, and white staves – stood to attention on each side of the Queen Victoria Memorial statue as the Lord Mayor, R. J. McMordie MP, the councillors in their scarlet and ermine robes, the civic mace bearers and other city dignitaries greeted Sir Edward. Carson, with Captain Read still before him, entered the vestibule and advanced towards a circular table directly under the dome rising 173 feet above him. He took up the silver square-sided pen made by Sharman D. Neill of 22 Donegall Place and presented to him the evening before. It bore the inscription: 'With this pen I, Edward Carson, signed Ulster's Solemn League and Covenant, in the City Hall, Belfast, on Ulster Day, Saturday 28th September, 1912.'

When Carson re-emerged the reverential hum in the vast crowd outside changed to tempestuous cheering as he made his way bowing and waving down Donegall Place to Royal Avenue where he was to be the guest of the Ulster Reform Club for luncheon. Behind him the stewards struggled to regulate the flow of men eager to sign the Covenant in the City Hall. A double row of desks stretching right round the building made it possible for 550 to sign simultaneously. All over Ulster men were signing to pledge themselves to use 'all means which may be found necessary to defeat the present conspiracy to set up a Home Rule Parliament in Ireland'. At 2.30 pm a procession of bands from every Protestant quarter of Belfast converged on the City Hall. As each contingent arrived the bandsmen halted at a prearranged position in Donegall Square, all continuing to play different tunes, creating, in the opinion of the *Northern Whig*, 'a fine post-impressionist effect about it that should have pleased admirers of the new style of music'. J. L. Garvin, reporting for the *Pall Mall Gazette* wrote:

Seen from the topmost outside gallery of the dome, the square below, and the streets striking away from it were black with people. Through the mass, with drums and fifes, sashes and banners, the clubs marched all day. The streets surged with cheering, but still no policemen, still no shouts of rage or insult . . .

It was 8 pm when the last contingent entered the City Hall and signatures were still being affixed after 11 pm.

Huge crowds sang 'Rule Britannia' and 'God save the King' as Carson and the Unionist leaders walked round the corner from the Ulster Reform Club in Royal Avenue to the Ulster Club in Castle Place. Trams had to be diverted and jarveys were forced to take their horses away from the Bank Buildings to a place of safety. At 8.30 pm a brass band advanced towards the Ulster Club playing 'See the conquering hero comes', its staff major and spear carriers almost having to carve a way through the surging mass. A searchlight from the Olde Castle Restaurant played on the scene and deafening cheers greeted Carson when he came out of the club and with twenty other dignitaries climbed into a waiting motor brake designed for twelve passengers. Lord Londonderry, swept off his feet, temporarily got lost in the crowd. The vehicle was pulled down High Street by hundreds of willing hands. 'With a roaring hurricane of cheers punctuated on every side by the steady rattle of revolver shots,' Garvin wrote, 'onward swept this whole city in motion with a tumult that was mad.'

Another enormous crowd was waiting at the Belfast Steamship Company's

shed on Donegall Quay; many clung to perilous perches on cranes and lampposts. Sir Edward was saluted by a fusillade of shots and prolonged cheering. Bonfires in Great Patrick Street sprang to life and a huge fire on the Cave Hill threw a brilliant glare over the sky. After making a short speech, Carson was welcomed aboard the *Patriotic* by Captain John Paisley, and from the upper deck, the *Belfast News-Letter* reported, he shouted out: 'I have very little voice left. I ask you while I am away in England and Scotland and fighting your battle in the Imperial Parliament to keep the old flag flying. (Cheers.) And "No Surrender!" (Loud Cheers.).'

All over Ulster men were signing the Covenant and women separately signed their own declaration. Altogether 471,414 people signed. Except for some scuffles at Grosvenor Park where Celtic beat Distillery, there had been no violence in the city that day. Covenant Day was denounced as 'a silly masquerade' by the *Irish News*, the Ulster newspaper for the Nationalists, and as 'an impressive farce' by the *Freeman's Journal*, while the *Manchester Guardian* contrasted 'the anarchic hectoring of the ascendancy party and the loyal patient reliance of the Ulster Nationalists upon English justice and firmness'. The ecstatic Unionists, however, did not doubt the justice of their cause as they sang 'Come Back to Erin', and, as the *Patriotic* steamed into the Victoria Channel, salvoes of rockets shot up to the sky and fifty bonfires blazed from the hills and headlands.

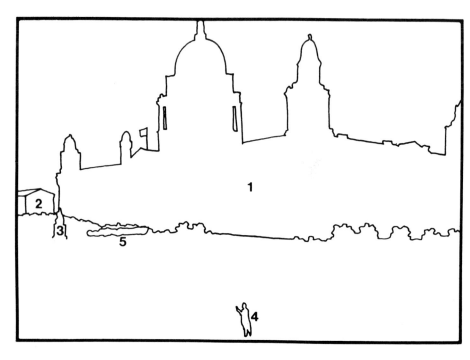

Looking south-east from Donegall Square North

1 Belfast City Hall, completed in 1906
2 Donegall Square Methodist Church, built in 1847
3 Queen Victoria Memorial
4 Sir Edward Carson, bareheaded
5 The Corporation in their robes

12 The Troubles in Ballymacarrett

In the first hours of Thursday 26 August 1920 the fire engines were once more racing through the streets of east Belfast. Flames were leaping up from spirit groceries in Isoline Street, Lord Street, Ravensdale Street and Avoniel Road. Hostile crowds still surged about in the darkness, and small boys dashed into the streets of their neighbours, smashing windows. The crash of shattering glass, the snapping of burning wood and the shouts of contending mobs were punctuated by the sound of gunfire. As the exhausted rioters retreated home, peace returned for a time to Ballymacarrett. Soldiers of the Norfolk Regiment, the Somerset Light Infantry, and the Duke of Cornwall's Light Infantry mounted a heavy guard on St Matthew's Catholic Church – the object of repeated attacks the day before – and stood posted at the street corners. Dawn revealed the destruction and violence of that night – cobblestones strewn about the lower Newtownards Road, charred shells of burned-out stores, overturned barbed wire barricades and a sea of glass fragments and shipyard rivet-ends known as 'Island confetti'. Between 7 pm the previous evening and 1.30 am there had been no fewer than twenty-four malicious fires in this small congested area.

It was still early in the morning when people were seen looting in the vicinity of Dee Street. The troops fired a volley: a nineteen-year-old youth was killed, shot through the lung, and a twenty-year-old girl, hit in the stomach, was mortally wounded. Peace followed only for a time. The people of the Catholic enclave of Short Strand felt beleaguered and angry: a month before, many of them had been driven out of the neighbouring shipyards and other major firms in the city. They saw themselves marooned on a Catholic island in the midst of a hostile Protestant sea. Protestants saw them as supporters of the widening guerrilla campaign being waged by the IRA against the British government.

The violence in east Belfast had begun on 21 July. As Rev. John Redmond, Church of Ireland Vicar of Ballymacarrett, recalled in his memoirs:

> . . . riots broke out in the shipyards in our Parish. The Protestant workers rose up and drove out all the Sinn Fein workers, who fled helter skelter. I have no doubt there were a number of decent Roman Catholics who did not deserve this treatment, but they could not be separated from the others . . .

A committee headed by the Catholic Bishop (later Cardinal), Dr MacRory, estimated that 10,000 men and 1,000 women had been expelled from their work. Repeated attempts were made to drive Catholics from their homes, and part of St Matthew's had been burned. The murder of RIC District Inspector O. R. Swanzy in Lisburn on 22 August sparked off another fierce bout of rioting which reached a peak on 26 August.

By the middle of the morning large crowds gathered at the Short Strand end of the Newtownards Road. A few baton charges dispersed the mobs for a time, but at dinner hour intermittent stone-throwing began again, McCloskey's spirit grocery at the corner of Westbourne Street was set ablaze and fires were started in premises looted and wrecked the night before. Troops strengthened the guard on St Matthew's and strung out a barbed wire entanglement across the end of Seaforde Street.

Only a few streets up the Newtownards Road from St Matthew's, the Rev. Redmond called a meeting that afternoon at St Patrick's School attached to his church. His basic sympathies were with his Protestant parishioners, and he was not sorry to see the closing of spirit groceries which were 'the ruination

24

of many women and homes', the owners being 'nearly all Roman Catholics who were regarded, not without some reason, as Sinn Feiners . . .' He was against anarchy and wanton destruction, however, and now he enrolled ex-servicemen as special constables, while his curates, Major Rev. Frederick Chestnutt-Chesney and Rev. J. E. Haddick, handed out badges and batons. The Lord Mayor, W. F. Coates, had given his approval; also present were Major-General Sir E. G. T. Bainbridge, the RIC Police Commissioner, and John Gray RM, who had come hot foot from the Belfast Police Court where he had refused bail to a string of handcuffed rioters. It was to be more than two months before the Westminster government agreed to establish a special constabulary under its own direction.

Redmond's volunteers could do little to contain the worsening violence. From 2 pm onwards fierce stone-throwing battles raged between Catholics in Seaforde Street and Protestants making forays from the railway embankment. The lower end of the Newtownards Road was littered with kidney pavers 'of which tons were dug up from side streets as ammunition', the *Northern Whig* reported. Driven back, the police called in the Army. While an armoured car fired occasional volleys, troops attempted, with limited success, to separate the combatants with a bayonet charge. The fire brigade, attempting to get at a blaze in Middlepath Street, had to run the gauntlet of missiles hurled by both sides. Several rioters were severely wounded when the soldiers cleared the streets with rifle fire. By 5 pm, however, the crowds were back in force.

At six o'clock the shipyard workers poured out of Harland & Wolff, and, according to the Protestant newspapers, as they marched along the Newtownards Road they were taunted and stoned by Catholics from behind the barbed wire at the Seaforde Street junction. Sweeping the obstruction aside, the shipwrights retaliated in force. The troops returned with an armoured car to cries of 'We don't snipe you boys!', and cheering by loyalists waving Union Jacks. Protestants used the car as a screen: 'They seemed to have petrol in plenty,' the *Irish News* reported, 'and all the materials necessary for carrying out systematic incendiarism, and they were also evidently well-armed with revolvers.' Then concentrated rifle fire cleared the street. Meanwhile more spirit groceries had been set ablaze, including Brownes in Kathleen Street, McCannons in Canton Street, Fitzpatricks at the corner of Templemore Street, and Megarittys of Templemore Avenue. The fire brigade, overstretched and its men exhausted from the night before, could save few of these premises. Soon afterwards O'Kane's funeral parlour, at the corner of Seaforde Street, and Lennon's spirit grocery on the opposite corner, blazed up in the biggest conflagration so far. As the *Belfast Telegraph* correspondent wrote:

> Tense excitement continued to prevail. Numerous bonfires were lighted, looted property being wantonly burned. In Dee Street a spirit grocery was fired, while in Pitt Street a huge pile of furniture taken from one of the residences was set on fire and burned furiously for several hours.

The *Belfast News-Letter* observed that around these fires 'crowds of young people gathered, singing and dancing'. It was now almost dark, and Rev. Redmond, his curates and his constables kept a mob at bay in front of Murray's public house on the corner of Templemore Avenue and the Newtownards Road. At 11 pm there was shooting from Memel Street and Seaforde Street and the Protestants – seeing that the special constables had

gone – set fire to Murrays, the flames of the three-storey building illuminating the whole district. At the same time the military post at Bridge End was attacked by men with revolvers. Soldiers returned the fire; Francis McCann, of Chemical Street, was shot dead and Patrick Young, of Foundry Street, was wounded in the leg. The turmoil ceased finally at midnight when, the *Irish News* reported in heavy type, 'the Newtownards Road was absolutely swept by machine gun and rifle fire in both directions'.

The long vigil of the Very Rev. Father Crolly and the priests of St Matthew's was over. They considered it fortunate that no more than two stained-glass windows had been broken by flying missiles. Indeed it was remarkable that only three people had been killed that day, though there had been intense rioting and shooting in west Belfast also – in Cupar Street, Kashmir Road, Albert Street and Durham Street. The fighting and destruction had only begun. For the next two years sectarian conflict raged, and as a result of assassinations, expulsions, bomb attacks, street rioting and house burnings 453 were killed in the city – 257 Catholics, 157 Protestants, 2 of unknown religion, and 37 soldiers and police.

At the close of 1920 the postwar boom shuddered to a halt. For the next two decades a deep slump settled on Belfast and around one quarter of insured workers were unemployed until the renewal of international conflict.

Looking from Lower Newtownards Road along Seaforde Street

1 Seaforde Street
2 Lower Newtownards Road
3 A Lancia armoured car
4 O'Kane's Funeral Furnishers
5 Lennon's Spirit Grocery

13 The Belfast Blitz

Easter Tuesday had been a dull oppressive day but the sky was clearing that evening as 180 German bombers, predominantly Junkers 88s and Heinkel 111s, flew in formation over the Irish Sea. The crews had closely studied photographs taken five months before by a *Luftwaffe* reconnaissance aeroplane, and they had memorised their principal targets '. . . *die Werft Harland & Wolff Ltd., die Tankskelle Conns Water, das Flugzeugwerk Short & Harland, das Kraftwerk Belfast, die Grossmuhle Rank & Co* . . .' Long presumed by both Whitehall and Stormont to be too far from Germany for concentrated air attack, Belfast was almost defenceless. There were no searchlights, no night fighters, only two small balloon barrages, only one RAF Hurricane squadron, only a few scattered and defective shelters, and only thirty-eight anti-aircraft guns in all of Northern Ireland.

As the bombers approached the Ards peninsula, they dropped to 7,000 feet. On the Castlereagh Hills ground crews manned anti-aircraft guns; Hawker Hurricane Mark IIs sped down the runway at Aldergrove Airport, and at 10.40 pm sirens wailed in Belfast. Casting intense light, hundreds of flares drifted down; then incendiaries, high-explosive bombs and parachute mines rained on the city. It was not the industrial heartland but the congested housing north of the city centre that received the full force of the attack. This was not the German intention: perhaps the Cavehill Waterworks was mistaken for the harbour; perhaps a hastily contrived smoke screen at the shipyards confused the pilots; or perhaps the instruction to take a bearing on the twin spires of St Peter's on the Falls caused the Germans to overshoot their targets. The result was a fearful carnage in the New Lodge, the lower Shankill and the Antrim Road.

At least twenty parachute mines, designed to rend apart the reinforced concrete and steel of factories and workshops, fell in the New Lodge. Veryan Gardens and Hogarth Street, off the Antrim Road, were totally destroyed. York Street Spinning Mill, the largest of its kind in Europe, was sliced in two; the collapsing six storeys obliterated forty-two houses in Sussex Street and twenty-one in Vere Street. Over sixty people died when a bomb fell next to a shelter in Percy Street. In one house in Ballynure Street sixteen were killed, nine from one family. Altogether 203 metric tons of bombs and 800 fire-bomb canisters were dropped on Belfast.

At 1.45 am, a bomb fell at the corner of Oxford Street and East Bridge Street, wrecking the city's central telephone exchange. All contact with Britain and the anti-aircraft operations control room was cut off. The guns on the ground fell silent for fear of shooting down the Hurricane fighters, which, with cruel irony, had been withdrawn shortly before by Fighter Command. For another two hours the German aircraft attacked Belfast completely unopposed. Bombs fell at an average of one every minute.

Around 140 fires now raged in the city and several of these spread into conflagrations. Just as the Auxiliary Fire Service arrived to fight the great inferno sweeping across the Antrim Road, the water pressure fell away – the water mains had been cracked in thirty places. From his house in suburban east Belfast J. C. MacDermott, the Minister of Public Security, watched the flames enveloping the city. As he heard the crash of his windows shattering he crawled under his desk and, at about 1.30 am, he telephoned neutral Eire for help. It is likely that he asked Cardinal MacRory to intercede with the premier, Eamon De Valera. Soon afterwards Major Comerford, Dublin's Chief Fire Superintendent, was getting together thirty volunteers at the Tara Street station. Altogether thirteen fire engines from Dublin, Dun Laoghaire, Drogheda and Dundalk sped northwards.

26

As they approached the city outskirts the southern firemen saw smoke and flames rising hundreds of feet into the air. Horrified at the carnage, one senior officer in the Chichester Street fire station was found beneath a table, weeping and refusing to come out. In any case there was little the firemen could do to fight the flames – hoses were cut by falling buildings, fittings were often the incorrect diameter, and the water pressure had fallen too far. Some of the fires continued to burn for another twelve hours.

As dawn came slowly on Wednesday 16 April a thick yellow pall covered the city. Exhausted air-raid wardens, firemen and ambulance men tore at the smouldering rubble to bring the trapped, dead and injured to the surface. 'We wrestled with street doors blown halfway down hallways,' Sam Hanna Bell remembered. 'From under the stairs of a house we extricated an old woman still clutching a miniature Union Jack.' The Rev. Eric Gallagher, then minister of Woodvale Methodist Church, helped to dig the bodies of fourteen members of his congregation from the ruins of houses in Ohio Street. The evening before he had called at a house and he remembered a five-year-old boy there. 'He sat sitting on my knee for some time, and we were playing while I talked to the family,' he recalled. 'I helped to dig him out of the rubble the next morning.'

On the Crumlin Road army lorries were piled high with corpses and severed limbs. Many of the dead were brought into the Falls Road Baths; as more arrived, the pool had to be emptied in order to lay out over 150 corpses. Andrew McFall, a swimming bath attendant, remembered:

> One coffin contained – all open – a young mother with her two dead children, one in each arm. One lovely girl of sixteen lay in a coffin in her white confirmation robe with blue silk ribbon and black hair . . . Another son was trying to get his old dead mother's wedding ring off, but this was impossible. We tried to get the lid on a coffin of a man with only a stump for a leg. Rigor mortis had set in and I had to force the stump down to get the lid on . . .

'Bodies of the poor they were, of the homeless poor, lying in their own shabby blankets,' Joseph Tomelty wrote later. There they lay for three days as relatives attempted, often in vain, to identify them. Over 200 bodies were laid out in St George's Market – only half the bodies there were eventually identified. Five days later the unidentified were buried in mass graves: Protestants at the City Cemetery and Catholics (recognised by their rosaries and emblems) in the Milltown Cemetery. There was even a shortage of horses to draw the hearses. William Wilton recalled:

> We lost 47 Black Belgian funeral horses in the Easter raid. They were killed by the fumes, not by the force of the blast. We let another 10 horses run loose on the road and picked them all up again next day. One of them found his way back to my own house at the top of the Ballygomartin Road in the early hours.

The official figures were 745 people dead and 430 injured. The actual total was probably much higher. No other city, except London, had lost so many lives in one air raid.

Some 6,000 people arrived in Dublin from Belfast, including an air-raid warden still wearing his helmet. Tens of thousands left the city for the countryside. 'Children clutched their favourite toys,' the *Belfast Telegraph*

reported, 'little girls carrying dollies . . . Many brought with them their pets, from budgerigars to tabbies . . .' Of those who remained, 40,000 had to be put up in rest centres and 70,000 given meals every day in emergency feeding centres – 'wretched people', the Right Rev. J. B. Woodburn observed, 'very undersized and underfed down-and-out looking men and women'. Every night for several weeks thousands left the city for ditches and fields outside Belfast. For a time the common experience of hardship dulled the memory of ancient hatreds – as Andrew McFall observed:

> . . . before the raids the Shankill was the Shankill and the Falls was the Falls and ne'er the twain did meet. But after that big raid at Easter half the Shankill spent their nights at the Clonard Monastery and it was amazing the transformation that really came over people . . .

One response by the Ministry of Public Security to the desperate situation was to issue this order on 19 April: 'Destroy all dangerous animals at the zoo immediately.' Two RUC marksmen were sent to Bellevue Zoo and, the *Belfast Telegraph* recorded, Head Keeper Dick Foster 'stood by with tears streaming down his face, as the executioners proceeded from cage to cage and despatched the animals 33 in number, and a vulture'. The animals included, unbelievably, two raccoons.

Looking over the city centre from the air

1 High Street and the Albert Clock
2 Donegall Place
3 The City Hall
4 St Anne's Cathedral, begun in 1900
5 York Street, leading to the Belfast and Northern Counties Station
6 County Down railway terminus, Queen's Quay
7 The Lagan river
8 Harland & Wolff's shipyard
9 Junkers 88 bombers

14 Bloody Friday

In the first hour of Friday 21 July 1972 a twenty-one-year-old Catholic, Anthony Davidson of Clovelly Street in the Springfield area, answered a knock on his door. As he opened it he was shot several times through the chest at point-blank range. He was the first to die that day, bringing the death toll from violence in Northern Ireland since 1969 to 454.

Sectarian assassination, the principal tactic used by Protestant extremists, was on the increase in the Troubles which had worsened since the beginning of the year. On 30 January troops in Derry had shot thirteen dead in what became known as 'Bloody Sunday'. The Provisional IRA intensified its bombing campaign. The Abercorn Restaurant explosion on 4 March killed two young women and inflicted injuries, some of them horrific, on 136 people. On 20 March a bomb in Donegall Street killed two policemen and four civilians. Loyalists paraded massively and angrily on 28 March when the Stormont government was suspended. While Protestants erected barricades, Catholics attempted with some success to exclude the security forces from parts of the city known as 'No-Go' areas. As people in fear tried to move to safety, a bitter dispute erupted over houses in Lenadoon in west Belfast, and there were protracted gun battles there in July between the Army and the IRA.

The morning newspapers on 21 July carried large advertisements announcing the introduction of traffic restrictions in the city centre 'to afford greater security protection to all concerned'. A map showed seven sectors forming a rough triangle bounded by lines running from King Street to Royal Avenue, Donegall Street to Victoria Street, and along May Street to Howard Street. The main arterial routes remained open to traffic as the security forces were 'anxious to facilitate the transaction of business and commerce . . . '

Later that morning the Ballyhackamore Post Office and the York Street branch of the Bank of Ireland were raided by armed youths. The weather had been perfect since dawn, helping to draw people into the city centre to shop for the weekend. A succession of bomb scares started the confusion of the afternoon, with office workers, shop assistants and customers pouring into the streets. Two children ran into the Smithfield Bus Station and shouted that a bomb had been planted and that they had been told to give the warning. The depot had just been cleared when, at 2.10 pm, a large bomb exploded in an enclosed yard there: over thirty buses were destroyed or damaged; part of the corrugated iron roof was thrown into the street; heavy metal doors, placed across the depot entrance after the last attack, were lifted off their hinges and hurled into the street; and houses in Samuel Street nearby suffered blast damage, some doors being blown in.

At 2.16 pm three men armed with submachine guns carried a suitcase bomb into the Brookvale Hotel, off the Antrim Road; the building was completely destroyed. Seven minutes later a bomb placed on the platform of the York Road Railway Station blew off the roof – a passenger had spotted a suspect suitcase just in time to give the alert. At 2.45 pm a car bomb at Star Taxis on the Crumlin Road wrecked nearby tax offices and damaged prison warders' houses. So far the bombs had caused only a few slight injuries.

At 2.48 pm a bomb in a Volkswagen driven into the rear of Oxford Street Bus Station exploded. It never became clear at what time a warning had been given. Two soldiers, who had just jumped out of their Land Rover, were killed instantly. This explosion caused frightful carnage: in addition to the soldiers, four people, including Jack Gibson, a bus driver from Crossgar, were killed. The wrecked cafeteria and adjacent buildings were now blazing fiercely and firemen ignored warnings of other bombs close by, to recover the bodies of

the dead. 'Police and troops carried plastic bags,' the *Belfast Telegraph* reported, 'as they went about the gruesome task of collecting the mutilated bodies, parts of which were flung up to 30 yards away from the blast.'

Also at 2.48 pm an explosion in the upper yard of the Great Victoria Street Railway Station destroyed four buses and damaged forty-four others. Two minutes later car bombs went off simultaneously outside the York Hotel in Botanic Avenue and at the corner of the Limestone Road; several people were injured and many cars were wrecked. Five minutes later a bomb left in a Ford car cracked the parapet of the Queen Elizabeth Bridge. In the next four minutes explosions followed at the Liverpool Ferry Terminus, the Ormeau Avenue Gas Department offices and in Irwin's seed merchants in Garmoyle Street. Six minutes later Creighton's Garage on the Upper Lisburn Road was devastated by a bomb left in a grey Ford Cortina; again and again firemen were driven back by the intense heat. At the same time, 3.05 pm, a bomb in a hijacked lorry went off by the Finaghy railway bridge and, on the other side of the city, an electricity sub-station at the corner of Hughenden Avenue and Salisbury Avenue was put out of action. Four minutes later an explosion on a railway footbridge at Windsor Park threw concrete sleepers onto the line. At 3.12 pm a bomb blast in Eastwood's Garage in Donegall Street set off a fierce blaze; hundreds evacuated neighbouring buildings as firemen struggled in vain to prevent the fire reaching the *Irish News* offices.

At 3.15 pm a bomb in a hijacked vehicle exploded at the Cavehill Road shopping centre. No warning had been given. Mrs Maureen Walker described the horror of that moment to a *Belfast Telegraph* reporter:

> Oh God, there was flames, and then when they seemed to have died away there was nothing but only glass and blood. The people all around were confused and they screamed for their children. Somebody in the hairdressers was blown clean through the window.

Another woman who helped the injured saw 'people lying all over the pavements. There was blood everywhere. It seemed that all those injured were women and children.' Three people were killed, one a mother of seven children. Stephen Parker, aged fourteen, was killed; his father, Rev. Joseph Parker, rushed down to help the injured, not knowing that his own son had died in the blast.

Nine had been killed and at least 130 maimed by the blasts that day in Belfast. Twenty bombs had been detonated in sixty-five minutes. As smoke, flames and debris shot up from each successive blast, ambulances, fire engines and police Land Rovers roared through the city streets, with sirens blaring. The ambulance and fire control rooms were thrown into confusion and, with buses destroyed, the railway lines blocked and several streets sealed off, all routes out of the city centre were filled with people rushing homewards on foot. On that still, but now overcast, afternoon exhaust fumes from vehicles caught in traffic jams added to the pall hanging over many parts of Belfast. Only the long, hard-won experience of the city's hospitals prevented the death toll rising higher than it did. At the Royal Victoria Hospital a *Belfast Telegraph* reporter saw the fleets of ambulances come in: 'There were the lacerations. There were the limbless. And there were the dead – men, women and children, their faces covered in blood, with others mutilated beyond recognition . . .' Many watching the television news reports were reduced to tears by horrifying pictures of firemen and rescue workers, as Alf McCreary wrote in *Survivors*, 'scraping up the remains of human beings

into plastic bags, like lumps of red, jellied meat from the pavement'.

The day of violence was not yet over. Up to midnight there were thirty-nine explosions in the province. There was much shooting as the Army intensified its search for arms and explosives in the vicinity of Shaw's Road. At Ardoyne over 900 shots were fired at troops between 11.30 pm and 1.15 am; soldiers claimed to have seen a total of twelve gunmen. In a fierce gun battle between troops and the IRA in the Markets four people were hit by stray bullets. In a stolen car at Forth River Road a man and a woman were found both shot through the head. At Cliftonpark Avenue a man was shot from a passing car, and at first light a man's body was discovered on waste ground at Liffey Street in the Oldpark area.

The bereaved Rev. Parker began a one-man vigil for peace at the City Hall, grimly totalling the mounting death toll day by day. The killing did not cease. The Army took advantage of the revulsion of feeling after 'Bloody Friday' to launch its biggest exercise since Suez – Operation Motorman. From 4 am on 31 July barricades were flattened in the 'No-Go' areas, particularly in Belfast and Derry. But the fighting went on, the destruction continued, more people suffered violent deaths and no political solution could be found.

Looking south-west from Laganbank Road
1 Oxford Street Bus Station
2 Armoured personnel carrier
3 The Royal Courts of Justice
4 Oxford Street
5 Chichester Street

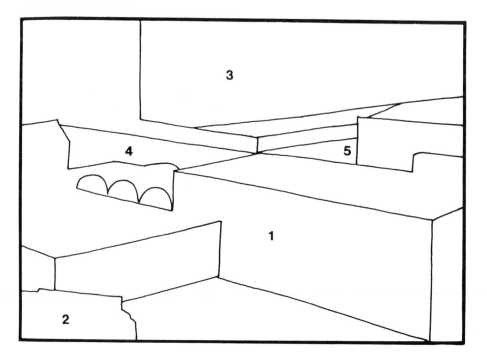

15 The return of Barry McGuigan

Monday 10 June 1985

On the control tower at Aldergrove Airport, building workers started to cheer and wave as soon as the aircraft began its approach run. By the time it had come to a halt, airport staff had surged out onto the tarmac, clapping and singing – they were welcoming the new featherweight boxing champion of the world, Barry McGuigan, who had thrilled millions by defeating Eusebio Pedroza in a fifteen-round contest in London. 'You have really done a lot to bring people together,' Alderman John Carson said as he pressed the victor's hand in the thronged reception lounge. As Lord Mayor of Belfast, Carson had made frantic last-minute arrangements for a civic reception because a fire in McGuigan's mother's home in Clones had brought the champion back days earlier than expected.

Driving to Belfast in a scarlet Lotus presented to him by a local garage, McGuigan was flagged down by an RUC patrol eager to get his autograph. Fans were gathering in the city centre and the rumour spread that the Lord Mayor had granted pupils respite from school that morning. 'Then,' the *Mirror* observed, 'Belfast, the divided city where Barry trained and filled boxing arenas with fight fans of every religious shade, showed how to lay on a real welcome.'

Outside the *Belfast Telegraph* offices in Royal Avenue the champion mounted a float decked out like a boxing ring; he held his infant son, Blaine, aloft to deafening cheers and his wife, Sandra, waved and smiled. While McGuigan's ebullient manager, Barney Eastwood, handed out bottles of champagne, Barry toasted his supporters with a glass of orange. Then, nosing forward with difficulty, the cavalcade set out for the City Hall. Fionnuala O'Connor of the *Irish Times* was there:

No city so needs non-political, neutral, preferably sporting heroes and few cities have more need of a good uncomplicated cheer. From the moment that apparently slight figure, carrying his little boy, climbed into the playboard boxing ring on the back of the lorry, the centre of Belfast shouted itself hoarse with pleasure.

Office workers threw down balloons and showers of confetti and sent streamers of pink and white toilet paper and adding-machine rolls billowing out over the street. Four men in office suits inched their way perilously along the roof of the Bank of Ireland to hang out their banner, 'Well done Barry'. As Blaine reached out cheerfully for balloons, McGuigan attempted to express his appreciation; the roar of welcome made this impossible and so he shadow-boxed instead. With relentless energy the Lord Mayor conducted the vast compressed crowd in the singing of 'Here we go', the banal words and tune taking on an anthem-like quality in the delirium of the moment. At one point, the Lord Mayor hoisted the boxer aloft and he in return lifted Alderman Carson deftly into the air to rapturous applause. 'It doesn't matter which side of the divide you're on. This fella makes you feel proud,' a man in the crowd said as 20,000 citizens cheered, chanted and sang in that congested thoroughfare, many reaching out in an attempt to touch or shake hands with their hero. 'I hate boxing,' a sociology lecturer declared to her companion and then threw herself ecstatically into the singing once more. In Donegall Place a photographer leaned dangerously out of a window, his companions clinging to his legs, on the second floor of C & A. The scaffolding encompassing the former Robinson & Cleaver building provided precarious perches for dozens of adventurous spectators; high up one man sat with his crutch under his arm. Fionnuala O'Connor continued . . .

30

by the time we reached the City Hall the champion had the look of a man who has shaken a thousand hands and this time might not go the distance. 'Looks dead delicate-looking, doesn't he?' said a girl wistfully. 'Wouldn't know him with his clothes on,' said her less wistful friend with a grin.

At the City Hall the champion shook hands with councillors representing every party except Sinn Fein, which had a policy of not attending city council entertainments. While a megaphone was sent for in haste from the RUC in Townhall Street, the boxer and the Lord Mayor eased themselves through a 2½-foot-square window onto the balcony. There McGuigan thanked the police, the Lord Mayor and the people of Belfast, concluding: 'Every drop of sweat, every punch I've ever thrown has all been worth it, and I'd do it three times over.'

McGuigan's triumph was the latest in a remarkable list of sporting achievements by Ulstermen, including Dennis Taylor and 'Hurricane' Higgins in snooker; Joey Dunlop and Brian Reid in motorcycle racing; Ormond Christie in hot-rod racing; Garth McGimpsey in golf; and Stan Espie, Sammy Allen and Jim Baker in bowls. As Mary Peters, the pentathlon Olympic gold medallist, had done in 1972, these sportsmen provided a unifying force in a city still bitterly divided along sectarian lines. Barry McGuigan's injunction, 'Leave the fighting to me,' was on many lips that Monday morning. Barry White, of the *Belfast Telegraph*, commented:

In the dark winter evenings, when the bad news bulletins abound, I'll be glad to think back to that snatch of summer sunshine, when Belfast honoured its new superstar, without reference to class, creed or birthplace.

The route taken by that triumphal cavalcade showed striking evidence of the recovery of Belfast's city centre since the worst years of the Troubles. No longer subjected to body searches, citizens were able to pour in and out of the security gates at will. Bright shops and boutiques had blossomed all along the thoroughfare and the only unsightly gap, at the corner of Rosemary Street, had been created by a recent accidental fire which had destroyed the Royal Avenue Hotel. Flower tubs, new paving and modern lamp standards adorned the main streets. At one end of Royal Avenue the *Belfast Telegraph* had built an impressive new extension, while at the other the Provincial Bank sported a plaque recording its 1981 Best-kept Building award. In Castle Place a new central Post Office – perhaps the most handsome modern building in Belfast – stood where the Ulster Club had been demolished in 1981, and in Donegall Square the recently-cleaned sandstone of the Scottish Provident Buildings and the Water Office gleamed in the sun.

There had been a remarkable revival of the city centre since the beginning of the decade, and between 1982 and 1985 forty-one restaurants, thirty-eight cafés and fifty-five hot-food bars opened there. Around £86 million was invested in commercial development in the inner city between 1983 and 1985 and it was estimated that in 1984 alone day-trippers from the Republic spent £120 million. Spending by the Housing Executive went up by 70 per cent between 1980 and 1985, reaching £545 million: attractive new dwellings, as in the Markets, Sandy Row and Donegall Pass, improved the quality of life not only for those who lived in them but also for others passing by them every day.

While the lives of Belfast's citizens were enhanced by the rebirth of the city centre, they were nevertheless diminished by a deepening recession and persistent violence. The collapse of De Lorean in 1982 and Lear Fan in 1985, together with the contraction of surviving firms, made the city ever more dependent on employment provided by public expenditure. Economic decline and sectarian bitterness contributed to the flight of one quarter of the urban population, principally to Great Britain, between 1971 and 1981. For seventeen years the city had been torn by the endemic violence of the Troubles, and the rapture uniting people on Barry McGuigan's triumphant return disguised, only briefly, the deep chasm separating the two communities. The recovery of the heart of Belfast rests on fragile foundations which could be shattered by a bloody confrontation or a few strategically placed bombs. On the other hand, the very harshness of the people's experience has bred a resilience and a hope, however guarded, that some unforeseen solution might yet emerge.

Looking north-west along Royal Avenue (same viewpoint as page 19)

1 The Bank Buildings, rebuilt in 1900
2 The former Provincial Bank, preserving the line of Hercules Place
3 The Reform Club, opened in 1885
4 The Grand Central Hotel, opened in 1890 and demolished in September 1985
5 Cave Hill
6 Royal Avenue
7 The new Post Office building, on the site of the Ulster Club
8 Barry McGuigan and party

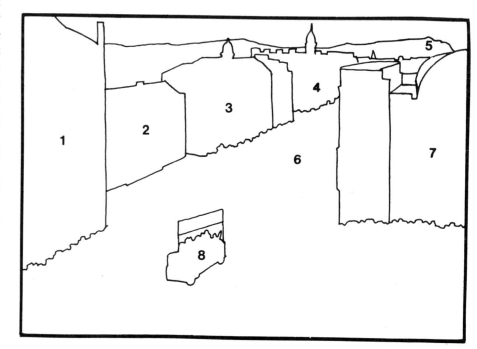

Bibliography

Olive Armstrong, *Edward Bruce's Invasion of Ireland*, John Murray, 1923

Jonathan Bardon, *Belfast: an Illustrated History*, Blackstaff Press, 1982
The Struggle for Ireland 400–1450, Fallons, 1970

David Barzilay, *The British Army in Ulster*, vol. 1, Century Books, 1973

J. C. Beckett *et al.*, *Belfast: the Making of the City*, Appletree Press, 1983

George Benn, *A History of the Town of Belfast from the earliest times to the close of the Eighteenth Century*, Marcus Ward, 1877

Derek Black, 'Belfast – The Great Revival', *Belfast Telegraph*, 16 May 1985

J. W. Blake, *Northern Ireland in the Second World War*, HMSO, 1956

Andrew Boyd, *Holy War in Belfast*, Anvil, 1969

C. E. B. Brett, *Buildings of Belfast 1700–1914*, Weidenfeld & Nicolson, 1967
Ulster Architecture 1800–1900, Ulster Architectural Heritage Society, 1972

F. J. Byrne, *Irish Kings and High-Kings*, Batsford, 1973

Gilbert Camblin, *The Town in Ulster*, Mullan, 1951

W. Y. Carman, *British Military Uniforms*, Leonard Hill, 1957

Douglas Carson, *Ulster Castles and Defensive Buildings*, BBC Publications, 1977

J. Cassin-Scott, *Costume and Fashion 1762–1920*, Blandford, 1971

Robson St. C. Davison, 'The German Air Raids on Belfast of April and May 1941, and their consequences', unpublished Ph.D. thesis, Queen's University, 1980

John Derricke, *The Image of Irelande*, 1581, reprinted Blackstaff Press, 1985

Richard Deutsch and Vivien Magowan, *Northern Ireland 1968–74: A Chronology of Events*, vol. 2, 1972–3, Blackstaff Press, 1974

R. J. Dickson, *Ulster Emigration to Colonial America 1718–1775* (for John Smilie's letter see Appendix F pp 289–90), Routledge & Kegan Paul, 1966

Peter Berresford Ellis, *The Boyne Water: The Battle of the Boyne 1690*, Hamish Hamilton, 1976

E. Estyn Evans, 'Rath and Souterrain at Shaneen Park, Belfast, Townland of Ballyaghagan, Co. Antrim', in *Ulster Journal of Archaeology*, vol. 13, 1950
'Belfast: the Site and the City', in *Ulster Journal of Archaeology*, vol. 7, 1944

E. Estyn Evans and Brian S. Turner, *Ireland's Eye: The Photographs of Robert John Welch*, Blackstaff Press, 1977

E. Estyn Evans (ed.), *Belfast in its Regional Setting: A Scientific Survey*, the British Association, 1952

Cyril Falls, *Elizabeth's Irish Wars*, Methuen, 1950

Robert Fisk, *In Time of War: Ireland, Ulster and the Price of Neutrality 1939–45*, André Deutsch, 1983/Paladin, 1985

R. Green and J. Cassin-Scott, *Costume and Fashion 1550–1760*, Blandford, 1975

Sybil Gribbon, *Edwardian Belfast: A Social Profile*, Appletree Press and Ulster Society for Irish Historical Studies, 1982

Thomas Henry, *History of the Belfast Riots*, Hamilton and Adams, 1864

Rev. George Hill (ed.), *The Montgomery Manuscripts (1603–1706), by William Montgomery of Rosemount, Esquire*, James Cleeland, 1869

Paul Johnson, 'Renascence in Belfast helps heal the wounds', *Guardian*, 30 May 1985

Emrys Jones, *A Social Geography of Belfast*, Oxford University Press, 1960

Henry Joy junior, *Historical Collections Relative to the Town of Belfast*, George Berwick, 1817

G. B. Kenna, *Facts and Figures of the Belfast Pogrom 1920–22*, O'Connell Publishing Company, 1922

Harold G. Leask, *Irish Castles and Castellated Houses*, Dundalgan Press, 1941

B. MacCarthy, *Annals of Ulster*, 3 vols, HMSO (Alex Thom & Company), 1895

A. McCreary, *Survivors*, Century Books, 1976

W. A. McCutcheon, *The Industrial Archaeology of Northern Ireland*, HMSO, 1981

Richard McMinn and Shirley Magowan (eds.), *Ulster and the World Wars: The Belfast Blitz – a sources booklet for teachers*, Learning Resources Unit, Stranmillis College, 1985

Mary McNeill, *The Life and Times of Mary Ann McCracken: a Belfast Panorama*, Alan Figgis, 1960

T. E. McNeill, *Carrickfergus Castle*, HMSO, 1981
Anglo-Norman Ulster: the history and archaeology of an Irish Barony, Donald, 1980

A. G. Malcolm, *The Sanitary State of Belfast, with suggestions for its Improvement*, Henry Greer, 1852

S. Millin, *Catalogue of Exhibits relating to old Belfast*, Belfast Museum and Art Gallery, 1937

T. W. Moody, F. X. Martin, F. J. Byrne (eds.), *A Chronology of Irish History to 1976: A Companion to Irish History Part I*, Oxford University Press, 1982
Maps, Genealogies, Lists: A Companion to Irish History Part II, Oxford University Press, 1984
A New History of Ireland, vol. 3, 1534–1691, Oxford University Press, 1976

F. Frankfort Moore, *The Truth About Ulster*, Eveleigh Nash, 1914

K. Munson, *German Aircraft of World War II*, Blandford, 1978

Noel Nesbitt, *The Changing Face of Belfast*, 2nd ed., Ulster Museum, 1982

K. Nicholls, *Gaelic and Gaelicized Ireland in the Middle Ages*, Gill and Macmillan, 1972

John O'Donovan (ed. and trans.), *Annals of the Kingdom of Ireland by the Four Masters*, Hodges, Smith, and Company, 1848–51

Rev. W. M. O'Hanlon, *Walks Among the Poor of Belfast, with suggestions for their improvement*, Greer, McComb, 1853

G. H. Orpen, *Ireland Under the Normans*, 4 vols, Oxford University Press, 1920
'The Earldom of Ulster: the Inquisitions of 1333', in *Journal of the Proceedings of the Royal Society of Antiquaries of Ireland*, vols 43–6, 1913–16

A. J. Otway-Ruthven, *A History of Medieval Ireland*, Ernest Benn, 1968

D. J. Owen, *A Short History of the Port of Belfast*, Mayne, Boyd & Son, 1917
A History of Belfast, Baird, 1921

Bruce Proudfoot, 'Further Excavations at Shaneen Park, Belfast, Ballyaghagan Townland, Co. Antrim', in *Ulster Journal of Archaeology*, vol. 21, 1958

C. D. Purdon, *The Mortality of Flax Mill and Factory Workers, as compared with other classes of the community, The Diseases They Labour Under and Causes that render Death-Rate from Phthisis, etc, so high*, Adair, 1873

Rev. John Redmond, *Church: State: Industry 1827–1929 in East Belfast. Vivid records of Social and Political Upheavals in the Nineteen-twenties*, John Aitken & Son, 1961

Rev. William Reeves, *Ecclesiastical Antiquities of Down, Connor, and Dromore*, Hodges and Smith, 1847

Report of the Commissioners of Inquiry, 1864, respecting the magisterial and police jurisdiction, arrangement and establishment of the borough of Belfast, HMSO, 1865

C. Rothers, *Medieval Military Dress*, Blandford, 1983

S. Sancha, *The Luttrell Village*, Collins, 1982

G. O. Sayles, 'The Siege of Carrickfergus Castle 1315–1316', in *Irish Historical Studies*, vol. 10, 1949–50

A. T. Q. Stewart, *The Ulster Crisis*, Faber, 1967

Brian M. Walker and Hugh Dixon, *No Mean City, Belfast 1880–1914*, Friar's Bush Press, 1983
In Belfast Town, Friar's Bush Press, 1984

R. M. Young (ed.), *The Town Book of the Corporation of Belfast 1613–1816*, Marcus Ward, 1892

Index

RIVER
LAGAN

River Farset

N

Blackstaff River

Belfast 1685

0   Feet   1000
M   300

a Market House
b Parish Church
c High Street
d Waring Street
e North Street
f North Gate
g Mill Gate
h Castle and gardens
i 'Rampier' or rampart

6 RIVER
LAGAN

Long Bridge

River Farset

Mill
Dam

Blackstaff
River

Belfast 1785

a Market House
b High Street
c White Linen Hall
d Brown Linen Hall
e St Anne's Church
f Donegall Street
g Exchange, at the 'Four Corners'
h First Congregation Meeting House
i Poor House
j Chichester Quay
k Smithfield